CHAPTER ONE: GLOBAL GROWTH

Frequently asked questions

Things you ought to know about population

One need not be a demographer to understand the basic concepts and issues of human population growth. In an effort to dispel common misconceptions about population growth in the US and worldwide, Zero Population Growth (ZPG) has prepared answers to frequently asked questions (FAQs) about population. What follows is information on current demographic trends, their social, economic, and environmental impacts, and ZPG's positions on several controversial topics.

Why should we be concerned about population growth in other parts of the world?

The environmental and social impact of population growth knows no national boundaries and affects us all. Population growth anywhere in the world ultimately has an impact on the entire planet's environment. Many environmental problems, such as air and water pollution and global climate change, are borderless. As our population grows, demands for resources increase, adding to pollution and waste. More energy is used, escalating the problems of global warming, acid rain, oil spills and nuclear waste. More land is required for agriculture, leading to deforestation and soil erosion. More homes, factories, and roads must be built, reducing agricultural land still further as well as habitat for other species, leading increasingly to their extinction. One example of the interconnectedness of our planet's environment is the depletion of tropical rainforests. Rainforest destruction is not only causing a grave loss of biodiversity, it is also upsetting the atmosphere's climate control capabilities. Sometimes called the 'lungs of the Earth', rainforests are obviously vital to all of us. We can

also be affected by political conflicts that arise from environmental refugees fleeing overpopulated and environmentally degraded areas in search of more benign conditions, or from concerns over the rights to finite natural resources like oil fields, water resources, or land.

Why should we be concerned about population growth rates of 1, 2 and 3 per cent a year? Doesn't that mean that population is growing very slowly?

Small percentages of very large numbers add up quickly. For example, the world's current population is estimated to be 6 billion, with an annual growth rate of 1.31 per cent. Yet, at this rate, 78 million people (more than the population of Vietnam) will be added to the population this year alone.[1]

Another way to see the impact of growth rates is to consider the doubling time of a population. In Saudi Arabia, for example, the population is growing at the rate of 3 per cent and if this rate continues, it will double in just 23 years. That isn't much time to build roads, houses, schools and sanitation facilities to accommodate twice as many people. At the world's present growth rate of 1.31 per cent, the Earth's population will double in just 53 years.[2]

(Note: In order to calculate the doubling time of a population, divide the annual growth rate into 70. For example, 70 divided by 1.31 = 53 years [doubling time for world population]. The 'magic number' 70 is derived from a logarithmic equation.)

Why are developing countries experiencing rapid population growth while developed countries are either growing more slowly or not at all?

While both developed and developing countries have experienced significant declines in their death rates, developing nations continue

During October 1999, world population reached 6 billion persons, doubling in size in under 40 years. World population is still growing at a rate of 1.3 per cent per year, with an average annual addition of 78 million persons during 1995-2000.

World population 1999

- Latin America and the Caribbean 8%
- Africa 13%
- More developed regions 20%
- Asia and Oceania[1] 59%

Population increase 1999-2015

- Latin America and the Caribbean 10%
- More developed regions 3%
- Africa 26%
- Asia and Oceania[1] 61%

1. Excluding Japan, Australia and New Zealand, which are included in the more developed regions.

Source: World Population Prospects: The 1998 Revision, Volume I: Comprehensive Tables (United Nations publication, ales No. E.99.XIII.9).

to have the highest birth rates. A country's birth rate is strongly linked to the extent of industrialisation, economic development, availability of quality medical care and family planning services, the educational level of the population and the status of women. The Industrial Revolution in Western Europe and North America improved living conditions through advances in medicine, sanitation and nutrition. These changes led to declines in death rates, especially among infants and small children, many more of whom survived their early years than before. Birth rates remained high, however, and soon the population swelled.

As these regions gradually moved away from an agrarian way of life and became more urbanised, large families became less practical and more expensive. Machinery was used more frequently to plant and harvest food, reducing the need for children as farm workers. Urban families bought food instead of harvesting it. Over the course of the 19th and early 20th centuries, birth rates dropped dramatically in these areas as people experienced the advantages of having smaller families.

Developing areas like Africa, Latin America and parts of Asia are still primarily agrarian; therefore, incentives for having larger families still exist. The fast-growing cities in developing countries are filled with young men looking for work, while many of the women remain with

their children in rural areas, providing most of the work for food production. Because the technology that improved living conditions was imported from industrialised countries, death rates plunged dramatically. As a result, these populations are growing rapidly.

In many countries, the low status of women is another contributing factor to high birth rates. Women are often denied educational opportunities and have fewer alternatives to their childbearing roles. Many people throughout the world wish to limit their family size but lack access to modern contraceptives, family planning education, and other health services.

Isn't overpopulation only a problem in areas where population density is high?

'The key to understanding overpopulation is not population density but the numbers of people in an area relative to its resources and the capacity of the environment to sustain human activities; that is, to the area's carrying capacity. In short, if the long-term carrying capacity of

---

As our population grows, demands for resources increase, adding to pollution and waste

---

an area is clearly being degraded by its current human occupants, that area is overpopulated,' according to Paul and Anne Ehrlich in *The Population Explosion*.

In areas where density is high, some effects, such as traffic and air pollution, are readily apparent. But other consequences of overpopulation are less visible. For instance, people in cities often forget that certain resources and services, such as oil, food and water, are provided by transporting the items from outlying areas. It is generally agreed that overpopulation exists if the activities of the current population are depleting the capacity of the environment to provide for the future. By this standard, according to the Ehrlichs, 'virtually every nation is overpopulated' because natural resources, such as forests and soil, are being depleted. According to recent statistics provided by the Population Reference Bureau, the Netherlands can support 1,180 people per square mile, but that country is a major importer of resources such as minerals and food. 'Saying that the Netherlands is thriving with a density of 1,180 people per square mile simply ignores that those 1,180 Dutch people far exceed the carrying capacity of that square mile,' the Ehrlichs write.

Don't we have enough food resources to feed many more people?
Already, more than three-quarters

CONTENTS

Introduction

Population Growth is the twentieth volume in the **Issues** series. The aim of this series is to offer up-to-date information about important issues in our world.

Population Growth examines world population growth and family planning solutions.

The information comes from a wide variety of sources and includes:
Government reports and statistics
Newspaper reports and features
Magazine articles and surveys
Literature from lobby groups
and charitable organisations.

It is hoped that, as you read about the many aspects of the issues explored in this book, you will critically evaluate the information presented. It is important that you decide whether you are being presented with facts or opinions. Does the writer give a biased or an unbiased report? If an opinion is being expressed, do you agree with the writer?

Population Growth offers a useful starting-point for those who need convenient access to information about the many issues involved. However, it is only a starting-point. At the back of the book is a list of organisations which you may want to contact for further information.

*****

of a billion people suffer from malnutrition. Although much of the world's hunger problem stems from uneven food distribution, to feed future populations, agricultural output levels must keep pace with the exponential population growth. While increased investment in agricultural research and technology may result in increased yields, unless population growth is slowed, food production shortages and environmental degradation will persist.

'For just how long can we feed this many people? Too little is known about the long-term consequences of soil and water degradation and species extinctions to be confident the earth's resources can be relied on to feed indefinitely any specific number of human beings, even today's 5.7 billion,' according to a report issued by Population Action International in 1995.[4] This poses a challenge since the report also states that between 1945 and 1990 'food production and other human activities' degraded nearly three billion acres of vegetated land, 'an area equal to China and India combined'. This means this land has lost its capacity to hold and supply nutrients to vegetation. Two-thirds of the most degraded land is in Africa and Asia.[4] Arable land diminishes as a result of soil erosion, which deprives farmers of plant nutrients, and irrigation, which deposits salts and other minerals that interfere with root growth. Soil conservation measures have been, in large part, underfunded and unproductive. Global soil losses are estimated to be 25 billion metric tons annually, or 4.5 tons per person worldwide. About 10 per cent of all irrigated land – about 50 to 75 million acres – is 'severely salinised,' while another 150 to 200 million acres are affected by some problems related to salinity and waterlogging.[5]

Is religion an obstacle to population stabilization?

Not always. Many religious leaders understand the consequences of rapid population growth and the need to stabilise it. Although the Vatican's position on reproductive choice is a critical barrier to solving population problems, many Catholics around the world do not heed the Church's official ban on modern methods of birth control. In fact, two predominantly Catholic countries, Italy and Spain, have the smallest average completed family size (1.2 children per couple) in the world.[6]

In Muslim societies, there are many diverse views on family planning. In *World War III*, Michael Tobias writes that many Muslims 'insist that family planning is inherent to the Qur'an itself' and that birth control is approved of in Islamic religious texts, although abortion is not mentioned in the Qur'an.

Thus Islam's influence over a person's reproductive choice depends on that particular culture's views on family planning and, to a great extent, a woman's status. Studies have shown that fertility rates are higher among Islamic countries, such as Algeria and Pakistan, where education and jobs are less accessible to women than in other Muslim nations, such as Tunisia and Turkey.

Urbanization, higher levels of education, expanding economic opportunities for women and availability of contraception generally have more bearing on a person's family planning decisions than religious doctrine. Also, research has shown that socio-economic factors may outweigh religion when it comes to reproductive choices.

How does improving the status of women affect population growth?

In many societies, women are valued primarily for their role in reproduction. In general, throughout the world, women hold little or no political or economic power, have lower earnings than men and are provided inadequate schooling and health care. Combining family planning practices with programmes that improve women's health, social status, educational opportunities and economic well-being are effective ways to lower fertility rates. The empowerment of women is a key to providing them with choices about their reproductive health.

For instance, although the state of Kerala, India, is economically poor, its low fertility rate is comparable to that of many industrialised nations, including the United States. Because women and men equally share a nearly 100 per cent literacy rate, affordable and accessible health care, including family planning, and educational opportunities, women have the number of children they want, usually two. And while many Asian countries tolerate sex selection and infanticide, resulting in a dearth of women, in Kerala there are more women than men, about 1,036 women per 1,000 men. The rate for India, as a whole, is 927 women per 1,000 men.

Micro-lending has enabled thousands of women, especially in developing countries, to begin a micro-enterprise and to become financially independent. One famous example is the Grameen Bank in Bangladesh, which lent to poor women, and received a payback rate of 99 per cent in two years.

Will AIDS 'solve' the overpopulation problem?

The main demographic impact of AIDS will be to lower life expectancy through increased infant and young adult mortality. Additionally it will burden health systems, increase the orphan population, change the social structure, and impede economic development, which may threaten economic and political stability in some areas.[7] The Joint United Nations Program on HIV/AIDS (UNAIDS) estimates that 33.4 million people worldwide were infected with the human immunodeficiency virus, as of December 1998. While AIDS will have a devastating impact in specific countries, mostly in Africa, UN demographers project that in demographic terms, the effect will be limited on the global scale.[8]

References
1, 2 *1999 World Population Data Sheet*, Population Reference Bureau.
3-5 *Conserving Land: Population and Sustainable Food Production*, Population Action International, 1995.
6 *1999 World Population Data Sheet*, Population Reference Bureau
7, 8 UNAIDS and the World Health Organisation, 1998.

Six key countries push world to 9bn people

By 2050, the UN says, 90% will live in a developing country. In Europe, the proportion of children could fall to 14%

Rapid population growth and relatively high fertility levels in the world's 48 least developed countries, and rising life expectancy everywhere, will help push the world's population from 6.1bn to about 9.3bn by 2050, according to a UN report published yesterday.

It estimates that the world's population is growing by 1.2% annually, or 77m people, and six countries account for half the increase: India, China, Pakistan, Nigeria, Bangladesh and Indonesia.

The population division of the UN department of economic and social affairs points to growing imbalance between the developed and developing world, the population growth concentrated overwhelmingly in those countries least able to support it. The 48 least developed countries are expected to nearly triple their population, from 658m to 1.8bn.

These increases, if realised, are certain to intensify pressure on food and water resources in many parts of the developing world, and they present an enormous challenge to international aid, poverty reduction and education programmes. They are also expected to exacerbate problems such as global warming and environmental degradation.

More international migration will be another consequence, the report says.

In the EU, increased immigration will be essential if workforce levels are to be sustained as the indigenous population ages, it argues.

'The population of the less developed regions is projected to rise steadily from 4.9bn in 2000 to 8.2bn in 2050,' it says.

By Simon Tisdall

Even this startling projection is based on the assumption that fertility will continue to decline. If that failed to happen, the population of less developed regions would reach an enormous 11.9bn.

Looked at another way, the UN figures suggest that within 50

> *It is estimated that the world's population is growing by 1.2% annually, or 77m people, and six countries account for half the increase*

years nine out of every 10 people will be living in a developing country. One in every six will be living in India where the current population of just over 1bn is projected to rise by 600m.

By contrast, population levels in Europe and Japan are projected to decline sharply because fertility is falling below the 'replacement level' – that is to say, below an average of 2.1 children a woman.

By mid-century the populations of Germany and Japan will have fallen on current trends by 14%, that of Italy by 25% and that of Russia and Ukraine by between 28% and 40%.

But this trend will be mitigated to some degree by more immigration, the report says, amounting to a net average annual gain in developed countries of about 2m.

'Because of low fertility, this

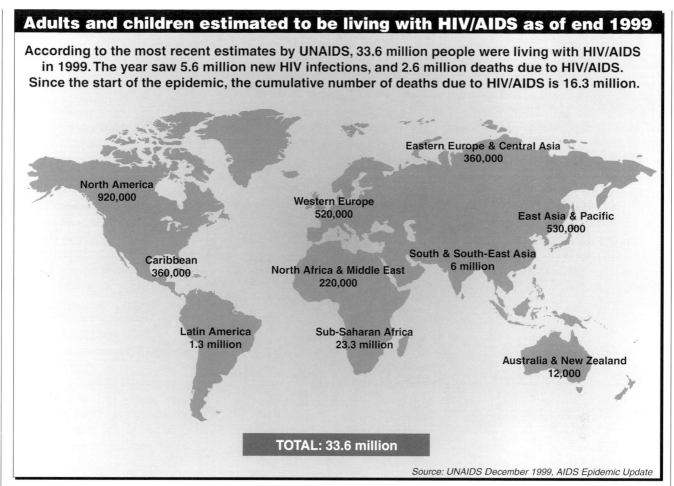

Adults and children estimated to be living with HIV/AIDS as of end 1999

According to the most recent estimates by UNAIDS, 33.6 million people were living with HIV/AIDS in 1999. The year saw 5.6 million new HIV infections, and 2.6 million deaths due to HIV/AIDS. Since the start of the epidemic, the cumulative number of deaths due to HIV/AIDS is 16.3 million.

North America
920,000

Eastern Europe & Central Asia
360,000

Western Europe
520,000

East Asia & Pacific
530,000

Caribbean
360,000

North Africa & Middle East
220,000

South & South-East Asia
6 million

Latin America
1.3 million

Sub-Saharan Africa
23.3 million

Australia & New Zealand
12,000

TOTAL: 33.6 million

Source: UNAIDS December 1999, AIDS Epidemic Update

migration has a significant impact . . . Without migration, the population of more developed regions as a whole would start declining in 2003 rather than in 2025.'

Britain, for example, has a fertility level of only 1.6 but its total population, currently 59m, is likely to be about the same in 2050, owing to immigration.

The United States is likely to remain a prime target for migrants, giving it an annual influx of about 1m people and a projected population by 2050 of about 400m; it has 280m now.

The report suggests that Africa, one of the areas of biggest population growth, will have three times as many people as Europe by 2050 – in all, 2bn Africans against 800m now. That compares starkly with the situation in 1950, when Europe accounted for almost a quarter of the world's population and Africa only 8%.

The population explosion in Africa, Asia and Latin America would be even more dramatic but for the impact of the HIV/Aids epidemic, the report says. But despite an expected 300m deaths in 50 years, the continent's population will still rise.

'For the nine most HIV affected countries in Africa, the population is projected to increase from 115m in 2000 to 196m in 2050. Even in Botswana, where HIV prevalence is 36%, or in Swaziland and Zimbabwe, where it is above 25%, the numbers are projected to increase significantly; by 37% in Botswana, 148% in Swaziland and 86% in Zimbabwe.

The population explosion in Africa, Asia and Latin America would be even more dramatic but for the impact of the HIV/Aids epidemic

'Only in South Africa, whose fertility is lower than that of Botswana or Zimbabwe, does the growth rate of the population become negative during 2010-2025, being positive thereafter.'

Although Aids has reduced life expectancy by three years in the 45 countries worst hit, the average human life span is still increasing there and elsewhere.

Futhermore, the life expectancy gap between rich and poor countries appears to be closing. In less developed regions, life expectancy will increase by 12 years, to 75, in the next 50 years; in developed regions, it will rise by seven years, from the current 75 years to 82. In Britain, life expectancy is currently 78 years, rising to 83 by 2050.

The prospect for the industrial world is one of elderly populations and shrinking workforces ever more dependent on migrant labour.

'The older population of the more developed regions has already surpassed the child population and by 2050, there will be two older persons for every child.'

One-fifth of all Europeans were aged 60 or more in 1998. By 2050 they may represent more than one-third of all adults, with children making up only 14% of the population.

Why population matters

Information from Population Action International

1. Slowing population growth helps poorer countries develop economically and participate in world trade.

When each new generation is similar in size to the preceding one, governments find it easier to provide roads, clean water, health care and education. The investment and economic growth supported by these services boost trade, which benefits the increasingly export dependent US economy.

2. Competition for scarce jobs eases when population grows more slowly.

Only extremely energetic economic growth can provide well-paid jobs to labour forces that are growing rapidly. Having a stable population – while no guarantee of full employment – tends to allow a better balance of job seekers and decent paying jobs. In today's global economy, slower population growth around the world can help support better paying jobs.

3. Migration pressures are aggravated by rapid population growth.

The search for work is the leading reason people leave the communities of their childhood. When job seekers exceed an economy's capacity to generate employment, migration – to a large city or across an international border – is a logical response. Environmental degradation, often related to population growth, spurs the movement of people as well.

4. Worsening water scarcity stems in large part from increases in human demand.

The availability of renewable fresh water is finite and increasingly constrained. By one recent estimate, more than half of all the world's accessible renewable fresh water is already being used, indicating the problems the world may face if population doubles. Within a single generation, the number of nations facing chronic water shortage is projected to rise to 50, mostly in the Middle East and Africa.

5. Worldwide, 800 million people are malnourished, and the number could grow significantly.

The food of the future will be produced mostly on today's farmland, and much of that land is deteriorating. Water scarcity and environmental problems limit the spread of irrigation. Slower population growth would ease the strain on limited farmland.

6. Humanity is rapidly changing the earth's atmosphere and thus its climate.

High energy consumption in industrialised countries is the biggest contributor to the build-up of greenhouse gases in the atmosphere. Developing countries are catching up, however, and population growth in both wealthy and less wealthy countries amplifies the role of rising consumption levels in human induced global temperature increase.

Having a stable population – while no guarantee of full employment – tends to allow a better balance of job seekers and decent paying jobs

---

7. The world's oceans are essentially fully fished

Despite the growth of aquaculture (fish farming), the global production and catch of fish have fallen behind population growth in recent years. With less fish available worldwide per person, the price of fish is rising. The world's poor face the loss of one of their few sources of high quality protein.

8. Wild habitats that shelter endangered plants and animals are giving way to human activities and needs

By the estimates of conservation biologists, tens of thousands of species may be disappearing each year – a rate thousands of times higher than is natural. The extinction of these species threatens the life system that humans depend on as well.

9. Disease knows no borders, and population growth is a factor in the recent upsurge of infectious disease.

By living and interacting in densely populated settlements, human beings make it easier for disease-causing micro-organisms to move from one host to the next. Crowding, travel and the increase of livestock – all associated with population growth – increase the opportunities for the spread of infection.

10. Civil conflict often emerges in societies where rapid population growth combines with environmental scarcity to undermine governments.

By contributing to environmental degradation and natural resource scarcity, population growth can play a role in tensions between groups. Governments often fail to resolve these tensions peacefully.

• The above information is from Population Action International's web site which can be found at www.populationaction.org

The numbers game

Information from People & the Planet

The rapid growth of the world population is a relatively recent phenomenon in the history of the world. The population of the world 2,000 years ago was about 300 million. For a very long time, because of high death rates, population did not grow significantly, with periods of growth followed by periods of decline. It took more than 1,600 years for the world population to double to 600 million.

Today, although the rate of global population increase peaked over 30 years ago, world population is still growing by over 200,000 people every day – the equivalent of a San Francisco every week and almost a Germany every year. The momentum of this growth derives from the huge numbers of people entering the reproductive age group who are now having children (though fewer than their parents).

Population increase picked up in Europe in the 19th century following health and hygiene improvements in the wake of the industrial revolution. But the very rapid growth of world population only started in 1950, with a sharp reduction in mortality in the less developed regions. By the year 2000, the population was some 6,055 million, nearly two-and-a-half times the population in 1950.

World population milestones
World population reached:
1 billion in 1804
2 billion in 1927 (123 years later)
3 billion in 1960 (33 years later)
4 billion in 1974 (14 years later)
5 billion in 1987 (13 years later)
6 billion in 1999 (12 years later)

World population is likely to reach:
7 billion in 2013 (14 years later)
8 billion in 2028 (15 years later)
9 billion in 2054 (26 years later)

Rates of increase
With the declines in fertility in most of the world, the global growth rate of population has been decreasing since its peak of 2.0 per cent in 1965-1970. Today, the world's population is growing at 1.3 per cent per year, with an annual net addition of 78 million people. The annual population increment is expected to further decline gradually to some 64 million in 2015-2020, and then sharply to around 30 million in 2045-2050. By then, the annual population growth rate should be quite low at a little over 0.3 per cent.

Ninety-seven per cent of the world population increase takes place in the less developed regions. In recent years the population of Asia has increased by 50 million each year, the population of Africa by 17 million, and that of Latin America and the Caribbean by nearly 8 million. Africa has the highest growth rate among all major areas (2.36 per cent), with some countries growing at over 3 per cent. Europe, on the other hand, has the lowest growth rate (0.03 per cent), with a negative rate of -0.2 per cent in Eastern Europe.

Changing patterns
Different demographic growth rates are changing the distribution of the world's people. While in 1950, Europe and Northern America accounted for 28.5 per cent of the world population, that share fell to 17.5 per cent in 1998, and it is expected to further decline to 11.5 per cent in 2050. Conversely, Africa's share of world population share rose from 8.8 per cent in 1950 to 12.7 per cent in 1988 and is projected to reach 19.8 per cent in 2050, although the impact of AIDS may not be fully factored into this projection. The shares of Asia and Latin America are relatively more stable at approximately 60 and 10 per cent, respectively.

© People & the Planet 2000 – 2001

World population growth

Top ten contributors to world population growth, 1995-2000
Net annual addition in thousands

No.	Country	Net addition	Per cent
1.	India	15,999	20.6
2.	China	11,408	14.7
3.	Pakistan	4,048	5.2
4.	Indonesia	2,929	3.8
5.	Nigeria	2,511	3.2
6.	USA	2,267	2.9
7.	Brazil	2,154	2.8
8.	Bangladesh	2,108	2.7
9.	Mexico	1,547	2.0
10.	Philippines	1,522	2.0
Subtotal		**46,494**	**59.8**
World total		**77,738**	**100**

Population of the major regions of the world, 1950, 1998, and 2050 (medium projected)

	Population in millions		
	1950	1998	2050
World	2,521	5,901	8,909
More developed regions	813	1,182	1,155
Less developed regions	1,709	4,719	7,754
Africa	221	749	1,766
Asia	1,402	3,585	5,268
Europe	547	729	628
Latin America/Caribbean	167	504	809
Northern America	172	305	392
Oceania	13	30	46

Source: People and the Planet 2000-2001

Population and human development

The key connections

Concern over the world's booming human population – which has grown from three to six billion in just 40 years – has abated somewhat as birth rates have fallen right across the world. But there is still a long way to go before numbers stabilise at perhaps 10 billion – and some countries, such as Pakistan or Nigeria, are on course to triple their numbers by the middle of this 21st century.

Globally, many experts are concerned that the earth's 'carrying capacity' is already overstrained, and worry that the huge impending increases in consumption in countries such as India and China will add enormously to the burden of greenhouse gases which threaten to heat the planet – not to mention all the other demands which increases in both population and consumption are putting on the earth's natural systems.

One of the complicating facts is that much of the world's population – especially in the South – is very young, with plenty of potential to reproduce. So that although the rate of population growth began to decline some 30 years ago, annual additions to the human population are still near to their highest level, with some 78 million being added every year, or over 200,000 people every day. This is equivalent of a San Francisco every week and almost a Germany every year.

These people all need food, housing, jobs and health care. And once basic needs are met, the appetite for other consumer goods and services seems to be limited only by the ability to pay for them. Human impacts on resources and on the environment vary, therefore, not only with changes in population growth and distribution but also with changes in levels of consumption and the technologies involved.

For example, since 1950 the richest fifth of humanity has doubled its consumption of energy, meat, timber, steel and copper per person and quadrupled its car ownership, while the poorest fifth of humanity has increased its general consumption hardly at all.

Making problems worse

For this reason, booming population is only one among many causes of social and environmental problems. But such growth can make these problems much more difficult to solve.

- Rapid or persistent population growth can force farmers and fishermen to over-exploit fragile ecosystems with damaging results. It can also increase pressures on local infrastructures and services. It speeds the rate of urbanisation, often leading to dangerous, overcrowded and unplanned settlements, with poor sanitation, a lack of clean water and disastrous air pollution.

- In some rural settings increased population growth appears to have stimulated new farming methods, but elsewhere it has resulted in the over-use of slash and burn techniques, and unsustainable land clearance on fragile, sloping and forested land and destructive coastal development.

- One billion new jobs must be created over the next decade just to maintain current employment levels. The availability of a young, educated labour force can be a bonus in newly industrialising countries, but jobs are especially hard to create in countries with high levels of underemployment, poor educational standards and limited infrastructure – and these are often the ones with rapid increases in population.

- Food production must increase 75 per cent by 2030 in order to feed the world's growing population. To provide a typical 'Western' diet, production would have to increase sixfold.

- Every year, some 27,000 plant and animal species become extinct. Most species extinction can be traced to human encroachments on habitat, including forests and coral reefs, which results from population growth and economic development.
- Where resources are already limited, rapid population growth can make it more difficult to eradicate poverty, because the economy, infrastructure and the necessary pool of teachers, doctors and other professionals all need to grow faster than supply.
- Although the percentage of people in absolute poverty has fallen from 28 to 24.5 per cent in recent years, the increase in population means that the actual number of people in poverty has stayed the same.
- More than any other resource, water shortage is becoming critical issue both for agriculture

and industry, causing tension between farming needs and city growth. A safe water supply is also one of the most important factors in improving the health of poor families.
- Human activities have destroyed 11 per cent of the globe's arable land, the size of China and India combined, and over 40 per cent is now degraded in some way. As a result, every year, the world's farmers must feed 78 million more people with 27 billion fewer tons of topsoil.
- Population growth is fuelling very rapid urban growth in the developing world. By 2030, nearly 5 billion people (over 60 per cent of the world's population) are expected to live in cities. And while cities have great potential to enrich life, the speed of their growth has led to immense environmental problems. Some 600 million

city dwellers are today without adequate shelter and over 400 million do not have access to the simplest latrines.

Among the many prescriptions for dealing with such problems, perhaps none has such a catalytic effect as the education of girls. This helps lower child and maternal mortality rates; it increases the demand for family planning and reduces average family size (or what the demographers refer to as 'fertility'); it increases the educational attainment by daughters and their children; it raises productivity; and it improves environmental management.

It is also one key element of the Action Plan agreed at the UN Conference on Population and Development agreed in Cairo in 1994, and further strengthened at a follow-up conference in New York in 1999

Health and ageing

Health and nutrition emerging and re-emerging issues in developing countries

Population ageing and the growing number of elderly persons are two of the most important demographic changes to emerge in the final decades of the twentieth century. An unprecedented proportion of the human population is elderly, and this share will increase rapidly over the next two decades, particularly in developing countries.

One billion elderly by 2020

The World Health Organisation categorises as 'elderly' all persons over age 60, which is half the maximum human survival age of 120 years. In 1980, 8.5 per cent of the world's population was over 60 years, rising to 9.4 per cent in 1990 and 11 per cent in 2000. By 2020, this age group is expected to represent one billion individuals – 13.3 per cent of a projected world population of 7.5 billion. Almost three-quarters of those one billion elderly will live in developing countries. In fact, 7 of the 10 nations with the largest elderly

By Noel W. Solomons

populations in 2020 will be developing nations: Bangladesh (with a projected 14 million elderly), Brazil (30 million), China (231 million), India (145 million), Indonesia (29 million); Mexico (15 million), and Pakistan (18 million).

The current demographic profile of a typical developing country, with high fertility and low life expectancy, can be visualised as a

In 1980, 8.5 per cent of the world's population was over 60 years, rising to 9.4 per cent in 1990 and 11 per cent in 2000

broad-based pyramid, with up to 50 per cent of the population 15 years or under. As longevity increases and birth rates decrease, this pyramid will assume an increasingly cylindrical configuration, with the over-60 population equalling the number of juveniles. This transformation will have dramatic implications for society, particularly in the areas of nutrition and health, for the first two decades of the new millennium.

Ageing individuals may be intrinsically vulnerable to undernutrition and its associated infectious diseases, as well as to excessive and imbalanced intakes and the concomitant risk of chronic diseases. The need for research that will develop empirical evidence to support policies and programmes to address the health needs of the burgeoning elderly population is critical.

Population numbers and trends

Information from the United Nations Population Fund (UNFPA)

Changes in the make-up of the world's population are unprecedented in their size and speed, especially among the youngest and oldest age groups, and in the rush to cities. Although the rate of growth has slowed, the ever-increasing population base means that a larger number of people continue to be added to world population each year. Over 95 per cent of growth is in developing countries.

The slower growth rates must not be taken for granted. Continued slowing of population growth depends on choices and actions in the next 10 years – by individuals, in government population and development policies, and through international commitment to reducing poverty and advancing human rights.

- World population reached 6 billion in 1999, an addition of a billion in only 12 years. Nearly half are under the age of 25.
- Population is growing at the rate of 76 million a year. More than 70 million will be added each year for at least the next 15 years.
- For 2025, UN demographers cite three population projections – a 'low' of 7.28 billion; 'medium' 7.82 billion and 'high' 8.38 billion – each variant based on slightly different assumptions about future birth rates.[1]
- The annual rate of world population growth peaked at about 2 per cent in the early 1960s. Since then, the rate of growth has gradually slowed to less than 1.4 per cent, but the ever-increasing base population means that the number of people added to the world's population each year has increased.

People want and are having smaller families

The trend towards smaller families has been greatly helped by the wider availability of good-quality, safe and affordable family planning services – and easier access to them, especially for women. Still, people are having more children than they want to.

- In sub-Saharan Africa, where fertility is higher than in any other region of the world, surveys indicate that women want fewer children than they are having.
- In Kenya, the gap between desired and actual fertility is two children. Yet fertility has already fallen in Kenya, from a high of more than 8 children per woman in the 1970s to under 4.5 children in the second half of the 1990s. Fertility appears to be declining in other sub-Saharan African countries as well, including Botswana, Lesotho, Namibia, (Northern) Sudan and Zimbabwe.

Young people: the largest number ever

There are more young people – over 1 billion aged 15 to 24 – than ever before. Among developing countries as a whole, more than one-third of the population is under age 15, compared with less than one-fifth of the population in the industrialised countries. The large number of young people in developing countries also could enhance economic development as they enter their working-age years.

- As these young people enter their childbearing years, this built-in population momentum means that, even if fertility fell

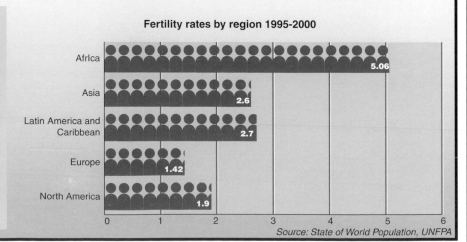

Fertility and population growth

Women are having fewer children than ever before – a global average of about 2.8 children each. This number – the total fertility rate – is a key determinant of global population growth in the future. However there are big regional and local variations in average family size, as the graph below indicates:

- Women are having fewer children than their mothers did because they have more choices – about education, employment, marriage and reproduction.

- Girls' access to education is of prime importance: among the 900 million illiterate people in the developing world, women still outnumber men by two to one. Girls constitute 60 per cent of the 130 million children who do not go to primary school.

- Female education has a direct effect on childbearing. The length of a girls' schooling has a direct bearing on the number of children she is likely to have, and educated women are better carers for the children they have.

Fertility rates by region 1995-2000

Region	Fertility rate
Africa	5.06
Asia	2.6
Latin America and Caribbean	2.7
Europe	1.42
North America	1.9

Source: State of World Population, UNFPA

immediately to the replacement level of 2.1 children, over three-quarters of the population growth currently projected would still take place.

- Since 1980, over 50 per cent of the increase in younger people has been in sub-Saharan Africa. In actual numbers, there are more young people in Asia because it is home to more of the world's population (60 per cent).
- In the least developed countries, the proportion of adolescents is 43 per cent of the population compared with 34 and 19 per cent, respectively, in the less and more developed countries.

A higher proportion of older people

Changes in the proportions of both younger and older people are changing the way populations are made up. Over the next decades there will be a gradual demographic shift towards an older population in all countries. People are living longer and healthier lives from infancy to old age thanks to basic sanitation, clean drinking water and modern health care. This drop in mortality (death rates have fallen by half since 1950) combined with longer life expectancy is a significant part of the story behind the fast population growth in recent decades.

- Currently about 74 per cent of the increase in the older population is taking place in developing regions. By 2011 it will be more than 80 per cent.
- By 2050, when the total population will increase by 28 million per year, older populations will be growing at about 33 million a year; with 99 per cent of this growth in today's developing regions.

The highest proportion of people aged 65 and older is found in Europe, and this will continue over at least the next three decades. North America and Oceania also have sizeable proportions of their populations above age 65. In the more developed regions, the proportion of the population above 65 has increased from 7.9 in 1950 to 14 per cent today and is expected to reach 25.9 per cent by 2050.

Africa and Western Asia have relatively low proportions of older people. In sub-Saharan Africa, the numbers of those above 65 will increase rapidly while their proportion will increase gradually because of the growth of the base population.

Demographic trends are diverse

Better health and access to contraceptives has contributed to a 'demographic transition' from high fertility and mortality to low fertility and mortality. In many respects, the less-developed regions are now about halfway through this transition, approximately where the more-developed regions were a half-century ago. Fertility is at or below replacement level in 61 countries.

A closer look at current trends, however, reveals a great deal of variety in the forces affecting population growth.

- Population is growing fastest in the poorest countries, those least able to provide for basic needs and create opportunities.
- In the countries most affected by HIV/AIDS, the situation is one of rising death rates and lower life expectancy.
- Migration and urban growth are also features of the current population movements.
- An estimated 13 million refugees have fled their own countries to escape from persecution, armed conflict or violence. Tens of millions are displaced within their own countries, many swelling the numbers of the urban poor.
- Immigration to industrialised countries may add to their population.

Reference

1 Figures in this section taken from *World Population Prospects: The 1998 Revision*, UN Population Division/DESIPA, 1999. For some regions, reductions or reversals of mortality declines (especially compared to earlier expectations) have contributed as well.

• The above information is an extract from the United Nations Population Fund's *Population Issues Briefing Kit 2000*. The kit is available on their web site which can be found at www.unfpa.org

Population not Taiwan 'is China's challenge'

By John Gittings in Hong Kong

China has singled out population growth as the key factor restricting its future economic and social development. It says it represents the country's number one challenge this century.

A white paper on population control coincides with the publication yesterday of a 12-point list of government priorities in which population pressure comes top and reunification with Taiwan does not even get a mention.

The white paper admits that China has 'a huge population but a weak economic foundation' and that although over 300m births 'have been averted' in the past 20 years by population controls, a net rise of at least 10m people a year for the next decade is forecast – a figure many experts believe will prove to be an underestimate.

The 12 'challenges for the new century' were published in the Communist party's organ, the *People's Daily*, yesterday. Top of the list was 'population pressure which will rise to an estimated 1.6bn [from the current 1.3bn] by the 2030s', the newspaper said.

The next priorities were: economic competition with the developed world; China's deteriorating environment; the need to develop more rational economic structures; and the need to reduce the gap between China's rich and poor.

The fight against 'world hegemonism and power politics' comes in at the bottom of the list.

But the population paper also strikes a realistic footnote, detailing a formidable range of social and economic problems which the Chinese government has barely begun to tackle.

It states that the sharp rise in the adult labour force has placed great pressure on the job market, that the social security system cannot cope with the number of people living longer, and that the gap between rich and poor provinces is hard to eradicate.

The white paper also warns that the increase in China's 'floating population' of migrant workers from the countryside – estimated unofficially at 150m to 200m – will make it harder to keep the birth rate down.

> **A net rise of at least 10m people a year for the next decade is forecast – a figure many experts believe will prove to be an underestimate**

There is an enlightened willingness to acknowledge the seamy side of modern Chinese society and the continuing discrimination against female births, warning that 'any action of maltreating, drowning and discarding girls is forbidden, and such crimes as mistreatment and trafficking of children should be severely punished'.

Help for female children, disabled girls, children in single-parent families and in poverty, and street children should also receive government attention.

International aid groups in Beijing say that over the past two to three years, their counterparts in Chinese ministries have become much more willing to discuss such problems frankly.

But they warn that obstruction at the local level, either through incompetent or corrupt officials, is still a serious problem.

In a candid assessment of China's current social strains, the white paper focuses on the need to improve health provision, particularly in the countryside so that farming families can ensure that their children will survive. It also calls for 'strenuous efforts' to check the spread of Aids and other sexually transmitted diseases.

The importance of education was also acknowledged as a vital ingredient.

'The rate of illiteracy should be further reduced', the paper says. 'The right to education of minors, women, ethnic minorities, the handicapped and poverty-stricken people should be protected.'

Planet Earth 2025

A look into the future world of 8 billion humans

By Don Hinrichsen and
John Rowley

Forecasting the future is asking for trouble. There are too many interacting uncertainties and too many unknowns. The Soviet Union collapsed only months after one eminent historian was predicting its survival long into the 21st century. Indian famines, forecast in the 1960s, have thus far been averted. No one quite knows how fast the earth will warm.

But some factors are more certain than others. Because to-morrow's parents are alive today, population projections for the next quarter century are reasonably predictable (although the HIV/AIDS pandemic has already had an impact on future forecasts). And related resource challenges are quite visible.

It is now clear that population growth in the next 25 years will not only take place very largely in the less developed countries, but most noticeably in certain regions such as South Asia and sub-Saharan Africa. Pakistan, for example is expected to add another 90 million people to its population of 146 million, while Nigeria could nearly double its numbers from 113 to over 200 million. By contrast, Europe's population will decline over coming decades. Some of the likely consequences are outlined below.

Food forecast

As the world's population grows to around 8 billion by 2025 – 35 per cent more than in 1995 – the demand for food and fibre will rise by even more as incomes rise, diets diversify and urban growth accelerates.

But, according to the International Food Policy Research Institute (IFPRI), if present levels of investments in agriculture and social welfare continue, food grain production in some regions of the developing world will only increase by about 1.5 per cent a year over the next two decades. Livestock production, it estimates, will grow faster at 2.7 per cent. But both these levels are much lower than in previous decades and will see population outstripping supply unless there is a big increase in developing country imports.

Even if this happens IFPRI believes that one out of four children under six years of age will still be malnourished in 2020. This is a slight improvement on the situation in 1995 when one out of three children were malnourished, but disappointing nevertheless.

But can this really be achieved?

Only, IFPRI says, if a big effort is made to improve the capacity of developing countries to enhance the well-being of the poor, improve research and extension systems, develop better management and markets and expand international assistance. A big effort will also have to be made to avert the consequences of widespread soil degradation, especially in sub-Saharan Africa and poorly irrigated areas of South Asia.

Liquid of life

One limiting factor in this equation will be the availability of water, without which the blue planet would be a dead and barren wasteland. Today, 31 countries with a collective population of half a billion people are experiencing chronic water shortages. Within 25 years the figure is expected to explode to 3 billion in close to 50 countries, making up more than a third of the world's projected population.

The main reasons for this are population growth and rising consumption. In the last half-century, for example, annual demand for water has grown twice as fast as population. Especially worrying is the overpumping of underground waters in countries such as India. According to the International Water Management Institute (IWMI), water in

World population by fresh water availability, 2000 and 2025

Fresh water is essential to health, economic development and life itself, yet there is no more of this critical natural resource today than in the distant past.

2000
Total population: 6 billion

- Relative sufficiency 92%
- Stress 5%
- Scarcity 3%

2025 (medium projection)
Total population: 7.82 billion

- Relative sufficiency 62%
- Scarcity 7%
- Stress 31%

Source: People in the Balance: Population and Natural Resources at the Turn of the Millennium. Robert Engelman, Rich Cincotta, et al. Population Action International, 2000

India is being pumped at twice the rate it is being replenished by rainfall. The consequence, it speculates, could be a reduction of a quarter in India's harvest, at a time when population there is increasing by 100 million in each decade.

Forest lungs

Another desperate concern is the continued destruction of the earth's forest mantle, which absorbs carbon dioxide and produces oxygen, anchors soils, regulates water flow, modifies climate and provides habitat for countless species of plants and animals.

Each year an area of forest the size of Nepal is cut, bulldozed or razed by fire. It is a process that has destroyed half the world's original forest cover of some 3 billion hectares, mostly in the last 40 years. Only a fifth of what remains is 'frontier forest', undisturbed by human activities, says the World Resources Institute.

And, according to a recent report by Population Action International (PAI), the number of people living in countries with critically low levels of forest cover could triple by 2025, rising from 1.7 billion to 4.5 billion or from nearly a third to over a half of the world's people.

Degraded land

Similar projections point to a critical loss of cropland per person, as population increases in some less developed countries. In Ethiopia, for example, where population is projected to grow from 60 to 100 million by 2025, the current 0.12 hectares per person will be nearly halved. The same factor is a crucial element in migration from the land and the rise in the number of 'environmental refugees', already numbering some 25 million according to the *Environmental Exodus* report by Myers and Kent.

The situation is not helped by the steady degradation of soils in many parts of the planet.

Worldwide, nearly 2 billion hectares of crop and grazing land, an area larger than the United States and Mexico combined, suffer moderate to severe degradation. To blame are soil erosion, poorly built

irrigation systems and other in-appropriate farming systems, including the misuse of agricultural chemicals. In the Philippines, for instance, nearly a quarter of cropland is degraded.

According to WRI projections, 40 per cent of the global population – or some 3 billion people – will live in land-short countries by 2025. In these regions there will be fewer than 0.07 hectares of fertile land per person – roughly the size of two tennis courts.

Death by breath

Population growth translates directly into more consumers of energy, more vehicles on the road, more industries and hence more urban pollution. The cumulative effects of population and income growth in the developing world and continued rise in energy consumption in industrialised countries are contributing to pollution and global climate change.

Today, over one billion people suffer from dangerously high air pollution levels, most of them in sprawling cities where industries and power plants have few, if any, pollution controls and where traffic jams are a perpetual feature of urban life. In 20 cities, most of them in the developing world, indoor and outdoor pollution is one of the leading causes of respiratory infections and premature death.

If trends continue, by 2025 close to two billion people will be living in urban areas with elevated levels of air pollution particulates, sulphur and nitrogen dioxides, heavy metals and secondary pollutants such as ozone.

Ocean planet

Today, just over half of humanity, some 3.2 billion people, live and work within 200 kilometres of a sea coast, on just 10 per cent of the earth's land area. A full two-thirds of the world's population are found within 400 km of a coast. Unbridled coastal development and mounting pollution loads pouring into near-shore waters have taken a grim toll on coastal eco-systems.

In the next 25 years, at least another billion people are expected to live within these coastal regions, putting pressure on coastal wetlands, seagrass beds, fisheries and beaches.

Of special concern are the 600,000 square kilometres of coral reefs, one-third of which have already been destroyed. It is estimated that within 25 years close to 60 per cent could be lost, as global warming adds coral bleaching to other pressures.

Losing species

One final challenge is the unprecedented rate of habitat loss and species extinction, almost certainly the greatest such event since the mega-extinctions of the Jurassic Period, some 65 million years ago. It has been estimated that some 50,000 plant and animal species will become extinct every year over the course of the coming decades. The loss of insects and micro-organisms is thought to be incalculable. Human-induced habitat loss and the introduction of exotic, or non-native species, has shoved the per cent of birds, mammals, fish, reptiles and amphibians threatened with extinction into double digits. Ecosystem destruction is so severe in the tropics that as many as 60,000 plant species, roughly one-quarter of the world's total, could be lost by the year 2025.

Of course, the future is always uncertain, and remains in our own hands to fashion, but the writing is on the wall.

© People & the Planet 2000 – 2001

Replacement migration

New report on replacement migration issued by UN Population Division

The Population Division of the Department of Economic and Social Affairs (DESA) has released a new report titled *Replacement Migration: Is it a Solution to Declining and Ageing Populations?* Replacement migration refers to the international migration that a country would need to prevent population decline and population ageing resulting from low fertility and mortality rates.

United Nations projections indicate that between 1995 and 2050, the population of Japan and virtually all countries of Europe will most likely decline. In a number of cases, including Estonia, Bulgaria and Italy, countries would lose between one-quarter and one-third of their population. Population ageing will be pervasive, bringing the median age of population to historically unprecedented high levels. For instance, in Italy, the median age will rise from 41 years in 2000 to 53 years in 2050. The potential support ratio – i.e., the number of persons of working age (15-64 years) per older person – will often be halved, from 4 or 5 to 2.

Focusing on these two striking and critical trends, the report examines in detail the case of eight low-fertility countries (France, Germany, Italy, Japan, Republic of Korea, Russian Federation, United Kingdom and United States) and two regions (Europe and the European Union). In each case, alternative scenarios for the period 1995-2050 are considered, highlighting the impact that various levels of immigration would have on population size and population ageing.

Major findings of this report include:

- In the next 50 years, the populations of most developed countries are projected to become smaller and older as a result of low fertility and increased longevity. In contrast, the population of the United States is projected to increase by almost a quarter. Among the countries studied in the report, Italy is projected to register the largest population decline in relative terms, losing 28 per cent of its population between 1995 and 2050, according to the United Nations' medium variant projections. The population of the European Union, which in 1995 was larger than that of the United States by 105 million, in 2050, will become smaller by 18 million.

- Population decline is inevitable in the absence of replacement migration. Fertility may rebound in the coming decades, but few believe that it will recover sufficiently in most countries to reach replacement level in the foreseeable future.

- Some immigration is needed to prevent population decline in all countries and regions examined in the report. However, the level of immigration in relation to past experience varies greatly. For the European Union, a continuation of the immigration levels observed in the 1990s would roughly suffice to prevent total population from declining, while for Europe as a whole, immigration would need to double. The Republic of Korea would need a relatively modest net inflow of migrants – a major change, however, for a country which has been a net sender until now. Italy and Japan would need to register notable increases in net immigration. In contrast, France, the United Kingdom and the United States would be able to maintain their total population with fewer immigrants than observed in recent years.

- The numbers of immigrants needed to prevent the decline of the total population are considerably larger than those envisioned by the United Nations' projections. The only exception is the United States.

- The numbers of immigrants needed to prevent declines in the working-age population are larger than those needed to prevent declines in total population. In some cases, such as the Republic of Korea, France, the United Kingdom or the United States, they are several times larger. If such flows were to occur, post-1995 immigrants and their descendants would represent a strikingly large share of the total population in 2050 – between 30 and 39 per cent in the case of Japan, Germany and Italy.

WHERE IS OUR NEXT GENERATION?!

...GROWING UP IN ANOTHER COUNTRY...

- Relative to their population size, Italy and Germany would need the largest number of migrants to maintain the size of their working-age populations. Italy would require 6,500 migrants per million inhabitants annually and Germany, 6,000. The United States would require the smallest number – 1,300 migrants per million inhabitants per year.
- The levels of migration needed to prevent population ageing are many times larger than the migration streams needed to prevent population decline. Maintaining potential support ratios would in all cases entail volumes of immigration entirely out of line with both past experience and reasonable expectations.
- In the absence of immigration, the potential support ratios could

be maintained at current levels by increasing the upper limit of the working-age population to roughly 75 years of age.
- The new challenges of declining and ageing populations will require a comprehensive reassessment of many established policies and programmes, with a long-

term perspective. Critical issues that need to be addressed include: (a) the appropriate ages for retirement; (b) the levels, types and nature of retirement and health care benefits for the elderly; (c) labour force participation; (d) the assessed amounts of contributions from workers and employers to support retirement and health care benefits for the elderly population; and (e) policies and programmes relating to international migration, in particular, replacement migration and the integration of large numbers of recent migrants and their descendants.

- The report may be accessed on the internet site of the Population Division (www.un.org/esa/population/unpop.htm).

© UN Population Division

EU 'will need immigrants' as working population falls

By Ambrose Evans-Pritchard in Brussels

The number of people of working age in the European Union is falling so fast that a vast inflow of immigrants will be needed to keep the economy running into the new century and prevent the collapse of the pension system.

Within 25 years, the EU will need up to 159 million immigrants to keep the current ratio between workers and the increasing number of retired people, according to a study by the United Nations Population Division.

Europe is caught in a demographic squeeze on two fronts. The overall population is not only declining – with losses of five million expected by 2025 and 40 million by 2050 – but it is also ageing at an unprecedented rate. Italy and Germany have the lowest fertility rates in the world, with their populations falling by 0.9 per cent and 0.8 per cent respectively.

Britain has a positive birth rate and is closer to North America in its demographic structure but even

Britain will face a serious imbalance early in the century that will have to be offset by immigration or an overhaul of the retirement system.

Italy's low birth rate means a likely fall in population from 57 million today to 41 million in 2050, a much faster collapse than the decline in the Roman Empire. While the number of workers in Italy will halve, the number of pensioners will almost double because of higher life expectancy. The twin effect will play havoc with the pension system.

Michael Teitelbaum, a demographer at the Alfred P. Sloan Foundation in New York, said: 'There is a different cause in each country. In Italy it's because women are delaying marriage and stretching the generations over more years. In Germany it's a long-standing collapse, and nobody really knows why.'

The estimates are in *Replacement Migration: Is it a Solution to Declining and Ageing Populations?*, to be published in March. The report says Germany will need 3.4 million immigrants a year to maintain the 'support ratio' of four to one between workers and retirees, a level that would alter the ethnic and cultural mix. Italy will need 2.2 million a year.

The need for immigrants could be reduced by raising the retirement age but the imbalance in the worst affected countries – Spain, Sweden, Austria, Portugal, Greece, Italy and Germany – is so acute that mass immigration is almost unavoidable.

Joseph Chamie, head of the UN's Population Division, said: 'I accept that all solutions are going to be unpopular but allowing migrants to come in is the only alternative to structural reforms that are simply too painful to contemplate.'

© Telegraph Group Limited, London 2001

Focus on urbanisation

Information from Worldaware

Our world is increasingly more urban, with people moving to the cities and towns that exist on every continent. People move to cities looking for new opportunities and a different and better life. This drift means that almost 50%, of the global population of more than six billion people, live in urban areas. This is continuing to grow at a rate of two and a half times that in rural areas. In 25 years' time urban areas will contain more than 75% of the world's population.

This rate of growth is greatest in the cities of the developing world, where there are twice as many people living in urban areas than in the developed regions. By 2015 it will be three times as many, by 2025, almost four times. Cities in Africa, Asia, the Middle East, and Central and South America are home to a third of the developing world's people. The developing countries already contain eight of the world's megacities, that is, cities with more than 10 million inhabitants. By 2015 there will be 26 such cities in the world.

In the cities of the developing world, it is estimated that at least 50% of the urban population has little or no access to clean water and sanitation. Other public amenities are virtually unknown. Their homes are in the vast slums and squatter settlements that have become part of the urban explosion. Unwelcomed by city authorities struggling to provide even the basic services, they are living amidst squalor and dirt, often the first to be affected by natural disasters, pollution and disease.

The cities of the Less Economically Developed Countries (LEDCs) did not start to mushroom until the late twentieth century. Migration, population growth and industrialisation provided the catalysts that have led to the huge cities of today. The lure of 'streets paved with gold' continues to draw thousands of people from their rural centres, only to discover the harsh realities of hunger, crime, disease and death in the large slums or squatter camps.

Urban morphology

The shape of most developing world cities is irregular, with a small high-class sector usually situated near the central business centre (CBD) or on a prime site. The rest of the residential housing is less well defined. Usually the largest zone is that of the ever-burgeoning shantytown development. Beginning close to the CBD, they have over the years spread outwards on the least desirable land. Often built upon wasteland or marsh, next to rubbish tips or sewage disposal

---

Almost 50%, of the global population of more than six billion people, live in urban areas

---

sites, their inhabitants build homes from whatever they can find. Gradually they replace these temporary structures with more permanent dwellings. The industry of such urban areas is stretched out along the lines of communication from the CBD, and often followed the movement of people to the cities.

The numbers of poor people attracted to the cities of LEDCs continue to increase, bringing with it an increase in the severity and scale of the problems that city authorities have to face.

Housing

The rapid growth of cities has overtaken the provision of low cost housing, the result being the development of shantytowns and slum dwellings. At present, there are 100 million slum dwellers in the world's cities. Shantytowns grow up wherever there is space. Using anything that is available to provide

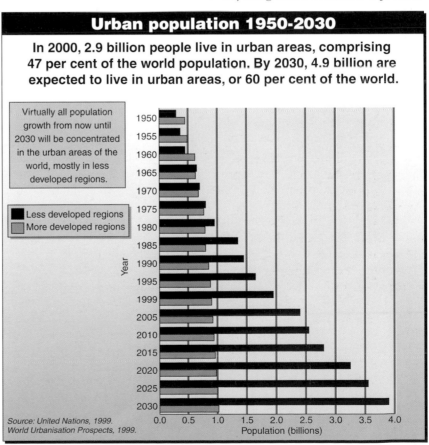

Urban population 1950-2030

In 2000, 2.9 billion people live in urban areas, comprising 47 per cent of the world population. By 2030, 4.9 billion are expected to live in urban areas, or 60 per cent of the world.

Virtually all population growth from now until 2030 will be concentrated in the urban areas of the world, mostly in less developed regions.

■ Less developed regions
■ More developed regions

Source: United Nations, 1999.
World Urbanisation Prospects, 1999.

shelter, these homes have no running water, sanitation, drainage or energy facilities. Often a number of people have to share one water tap and toilet. Open sewers run down the centres of the streets, carrying sewage that can pollute the water supply. With no rubbish collection, other waste lies in piles or heaps, scavenged by dogs and providing a natural breeding ground for diseases such as typhoid or cholera. Often overcrowded, extended families live together in appalling conditions.

Education and welfare services

The access to education has long been known as one of the ways to better social development. Whilst there may be greater opportunities in urban rather than in rural areas, there is still too little provision for the increasing number of children. Many remain illiterate, the families' priority often being that of using the children to help the family survive. Any children that do receive schooling will be encouraged to leave early for the same reason. Girls will be married off as soon as possible to reduce the strain on income. Greater emphasis is slowly being put on education, especially for girls, but resources are still scarce and parents need to be persuaded of the benefits of keeping children at school.

The increased number of people puts an enormous strain on the already overworked health services. While it has been shown that good health care can reduce population growth and ultimately enhance the living conditions, further education is needed to bring about a change. Many people find the cost of health care expensive, far away and they are too busy to use it. There is little money for good food, and diets are poor. The globalisation of fast-food chains has discouraged many people from even attempting to grow their own crops where there is land available. The resulting poorly balanced diet leaves children prone to illnesses, and infant mortality rates are high. Life expectancy overall is low. The impact of HIV/AIDS has left many children orphaned, living on the streets with no one to care for them.

Infrastructure

Only one-third of urban dwellers in Africa have access to running water, with less than one-tenth having mains sewerage. The problems for the city authorities are massive. Shanty-towns, or 'barrios' (Argentina) or 'bustees' (India), have grown up with no respect for town planners, and no provision for necessary services. Some cities have begun programmes to improve the availability of essential services. Progress is slow, and often hampered by inadequate involvement of the local communities. For example, this results in toilet blocks being vandalised as no thought was made as to who would oversee them. Road access is poor, dirt tracks that become mud slides in rain or potholed in the dry weather. Public transport to any available work in the factories is often too expensive and always overcrowded.

Employment

New factories have sprung up in response to the large number of people living in the cities. These are usually far from the shantytowns.

Wages will be poor, and the days long and hard. As many people are unskilled, they will join the informal economy, selling food, clothes, telephone cards, or even falling into the drug selling culture. Even tourism has its dangers for people employed in it. Some city dwellers may find work in the kitchens for exploitative wages, whilst others become enmeshed in the 'tourist industry' as prostitutes. The number of people living below the poverty line makes up one-third of all urban dwellers in the developing world.

The future

Despite the overwhelming lack of resources, life in the shantytowns and slum areas is not all despair. Celebrations, feast days, and saints' days bring life and colour and a sense of community. Projects involving the local inhabitants in schemes to improve the environment are having an effect. Governments working with NGOs and other voluntary agencies have started to achieve noticeable declines in death rates, illiteracy and population growth. More is to be done, but such schemes are part of the way forward in reducing the number of people living in poverty at the beginning of the twenty-first century.

• The above information is an extract from the publication *GlobalEye* which is produced by Worldaware. See page 41 for their address details or visit their web sites at www.worldaware.org.uk and www.globaleye.org.uk

Population and the urban future

World Population Overview 2000: Population and the urban future

Perhaps the most significant feature of the twentieth-century phenomenon of unprecedented population growth worldwide was the rapid increase in the numbers of people living in developing region urban areas. Cities and urban areas today occupy only 2 per cent of the earth's land, but contain 50 per cent of its population and consume 75 percent of its resources.

Europe and North America became increasingly urbanised in the eighteenth and nineteenth centuries with the advent and expansion of the Industrial Revolution. The rise in the numbers and sizes of cities in less developed countries, however, lagged behind.

Only two cities – London and Peking – had one million inhabitants in 1800 and the world's 100 most populous cities had a combined total population of 20 million. By 1990, the 100 largest cities had a combined population of some 500 million – 220 million in 19 megacities with more than 10 million people each.

Fifteen of these megacities are in developing countries. By 2015, there will be 23 with more than 10 million people, 19 in developing countries.

At the dawn of the twentieth century, the world's most populous cities were all in North America and Europe, but at the end of the century, Tokyo, New York and Los Angeles were the only industrialised world cities on that list. By 2020, New York and Los Angeles will no longer be included in the top 10 – pushed off by Dhaka, Bangladesh; Karachi, Pakistan; and Jakarta, Indonesia – and the only industrialised world city among them, Tokyo, is projected to be replaced by Bombay, India, as the world's most populous city.

The most rapid urban growth over the next two decades, however, is expected in cities with populations ranging from 250,000 to one million. The combined annual growth of such cities totals more than 28 million, but in another 15 years it will increase to 31 million.

The main attraction of cities is opportunity. In addition to offering the hope of employment with wages higher than could be earned in rural areas, cities provide opportunities for education, health care and a range of social services not readily available in rural villages.

Along with advantages and amenities, urban areas have drawbacks. The rapid growth of cities leads to substantial pressure on their infrastructures, manifested in sanitary, health and crime problems. Then, too, many rural-to-urban migrants lack special skills required in the trades and professions of the cities. Unskilled arrivals from the countryside frequently end up either in the informal job sector, performing menial jobs at low wages or resorting to begging or stealing. At least 120 million of the 2.8 billion people in the global workforce are unemployed, another 700 million are 'under-employed', working long hours, frequently in jobs that put their health and even their lives at risk,

The world's 10 largest cities

In 2001				In 2020			
City	Country	Population (millions)		City	Country	Population (millions)	Change from 2001
1. Tokyo	Japan	26.4		1. Bombay	India	28.5	53.2%
2. Bombay	India	18.6		2. Tokyo	Japan	27.3	3.40%
3. Mexico City	Mexico	18.3		3. Lagos	Nigeria	26.5	87.9%
4. São Paulo	Brazil	18.0		4. Dhaka	Bangladesh	24.0	86.0%
5. New York	USA	16.7		5. Karachi	Pakistan	21.7	76.4%
6. Lagos	Nigeria	14.1		6. São Paulo	Brazil	21.3	18.3%
7. Calcutta	India	13.2		7. Mexico City	Mexico	19.6	7.10%
8. Los Angeles	USA	13.2		8. Jakarta	Indonesia	19.4	70.2%
9. Shanghai	China	13.0		9. Calcutta	India	18.8	42.4%
10. Buenos Aires	Argentina	12.7		10. Delhi	India	18.5	54.2%

Source: Population Institute

yet do not even earn sufficient wages to cover their basic needs.

More than half of the urban inhabitants of Asia, Africa and Latin America live in poverty. More than 3 billion people – half the world's total population – subsist on less than $2 a day, and both the number and proportion of those living in extreme poverty are rising. Six of every 10 children in the developing world are projected to live in cities by 2025 and more than half of them will be poor.

City governments are unable to subsidise housing for millions of poor inhabitants, who live in slums and shantytowns. An estimated 25-30 per cent of the world's urban population lives in deplorably inadequate housing, squatter settlements, or in the streets where they lack sanitation, waste disposal and running water. City slums are breeding grounds not only for waterborne diseases such as diarrhoea, typhoid and gastroenteritis, but sexually transmitted diseases including HIV/AIDS, as well.

World attention must focus on urbanisation in poorer countries that will face high levels of population growth and urban migration. Nations will have to redouble their efforts to stabilise population growth at sustainable levels. While impressive progress has been made in reducing fertility worldwide, in some countries of the Southern Hemisphere women still average more than five children and levels of infant and maternal mortality and malnutrition continue to be high.

Developing countries will have to do their utmost to establish programmes to dissuade rural inhabitants from migrating to cities by improving the infrastructure in the villages and encouraging industries to locate in rural areas and provide job incentives for the people living there. Increased donor assistance from industrialised countries will be crucial in the effort to bring population into a more equitable balance with resources and the environment and ward off the devastating problems associated with urbanisation. The overriding priority of the twenty-first century will be to ensure the sustainability of the planet for the survival of the human species. That challenge, in turn, is inexorably linked to the sustainability of the world's burgeoning cities and urban areas.

• The above information is an extract from *Population and the Urban Future*, produced by the Population Institute. Their web site can be found at www.populationinstitute.org

Population and human well-being

Information from the World Resources Institute

Although the world's population is still growing, it is doing so at a slower rate than demographers had projected only a few years ago. Recent major gains in average life expectancy, reduced rates of child and infant mortality, and the increasing proportion of children now attending school all provide grounds for optimism about human well-being. Many of these gains have been made possible by unprecedented rates of economic growth in many countries. Some 3 billion to 4 billion people are expected to experience substantial improvements in their standard of living by the end of the 20th century.

Yet these global successes mask urgent, sometimes worsening problems at the local or regional level, especially among developing countries. More than one-quarter of the world's population has not shared in the economic and social progress experienced by the majority and still lives in poverty. Hunger, disease, illiteracy, and restricted freedom of choice or action are persistent problems in many of the least developed countries of sub-Saharan Africa and south Asia, as well as in parts of central Asia and South America. The pressure of population growth can contribute to human deprivation, especially in poor rural areas where competition for land and water can strain the capacity of local environments. Rapid population growth is also fuelling problems in many cities, where it can overwhelm the capacity of municipal authorities to provide even elementary services.

Yet the interaction between population growth and human well-being is complex and not a matter of numbers alone. The capacity of countries to support growing populations is enhanced when those countries achieve a sufficient, equitable distribution of wealth, technological development, effective government, strong institutions, and social stability.

More than one quarter of the world's population has not shared in the economic and social progress experienced by the majority and still lives in poverty

Population and endangered species

Population density, growth threaten species in vulnerable areas

The high rates of population density and growth in biologically diverse and threatened parts of the world further endanger plant and animal species in those areas, according to a new report by Population Action International (PAI), a non-governmental organisation (NGO) based in the United States.

Entitled *Nature's Place: Human Population and the Future of Biological Diversity*, the report states that more than 1.1 billion people live within the 25 most species-rich and environmentally threatened areas of the world. *Nature's Place* documents the historical impact of population growth on biological diversity on a global scale, with special attention to the current situation in these 25 'biodiversity hot spots'. All but one hot spot – a concept conservationists use to refer to areas where biological diversity is most concentrated and the threat of loss of species most severe – are experiencing net population growth, the 80-page report states.

Nature's Place reports that, while the hot spots cover less than one-eighth of the Earth's land surface, they now accommodate about one-fifth of the world's population. In 19 of the 25 hot spots, it adds, population is growing faster than in the world as a whole. In 16 of the 25, population densities are at or above the global average. Presently, the report adds, each hot spot retains not more than 25 per cent of its original vegetation – and most of them contain much less than that.

'We found that human population density levels and growth rates in the hot spots significantly exceed those of the world as a whole, a potentially alarming finding for environmental conservation,' said the report's lead author Richard Cincotta, an ecologist and PAI senior researcher. 'However, the current slowing of world population growth offers hope for easing the pressure of human activities on these ecologically valuable, yet fragile areas.'

The report finds that the human race population of 6 billion – its geographic spread, demand for natural resources, and ways of disposing of waste – underlies and fuels the more direct causes of recent and current plant and animal extinctions. These extinctions are proceeding at least a thousand times faster today than in the pre-human past. The rate is expected to accelerate in the twenty-first century.

PAI stated that its findings are in line with those of the scientific community. A 1998 opinion survey, it stated, found that nearly 70 per cent of the biologists questioned believe that a mass extinction is already under way, and that one-fifth of all living species could disappear within the next 30 years.

Among the regions covered by Nature's Place, population density is highest in the Western Ghats/Sri Lanka; the Philippines; and the Caribbean. Population is growing fastest in western Ecuador, the tropical Andes and Madagascar, it states.

PAI proposes a plan of action to help save a critical mass of the Earth's remaining biological diversity, including steps to ensure that people everywhere can determine for themselves the timing of childbirth and the size of their families. This, it states, will strengthen the trend towards slower population growth and, in turn, help the environment. Among PAI's recommendations are that the United States Congress ratify the Convention on Biological Diversity, an international treaty to save the planet's biodiversity and share its benefits. It also proposes that governments, donors and individual communities elevate the priority of biological diversity and invest in its conservation; and that donor and developing countries meet their financial and policy commitments to the Programme of Action of the 1994 International Conference on Population and Development, to ensure that family planning services are available to all who want them by 2015.

© United Nations Population Fund – UNFPA

Population and the environment

Information from Zero Population Growth (ZPG)

The link between population growth and environmental impact seems obvious at first glance: more people consume more resources, damage more of the earth and generate more waste. Humans are a force of nature. As nations develop, they increase consumption. This simple reasoning is true as far as it goes, but the larger picture is more complex.

- A very small proportion of the population consumes the majority of the world's resources. The richest fifth consumes 86% of all goods and services and produces 53% of all carbon dioxide emissions, while the poorest fifth consumes 1.3% of goods and services and accounts for 3% of CO_2 output.[1]
- Per capita municipal waste grew 30% in developed nations since 1975 and is now two to five times the level in developing nations.[1]
- An average American's environmental impact is 30 to 50 times that of the average citizen of a developing country such as India.[1]

The need is to balance the requirements of a growing population with the necessity of conserving earth's natural assets.

Human action has transformed between one-third and one-half of the entire land surface of the earth. We have lost more than one-quarter of the planet's birds, and two-thirds of the major marine fisheries are fully exploited, over-exploited or depleted.[2]

- Every 20 minutes, the world adds another 3,500 human lives but loses one or more entire species of animal or plant life – at least 27,000 species per year. This is a rate and scale of extinction that has not occurred in 65 million years.[3]
- Spreading deserts and declining water tables in a third of the planet are contributing to famine, social unrest and migration.
- Two-thirds of the world's population lives within 100 miles of an ocean, inland sea or freshwater lake: 14 of the world's 15 largest megacities (10 million or more people) are coastal. Their impacts include growing loads of sewage and other waste, the drainage of wetlands and development of beaches, and destruction of prime fish nurseries.[4]

Technological advances can mitigate some of the impact of population growth, and market mechanisms raise prices for some diminishing resources, triggering substitution, conservation, recycling and technical innovation so as to prevent depletion.

But market systems often subsidise industries such as logging, mining and grazing without tallying environmental costs. No market considers commonly held resources such as groundwater levels or atmospheric and ocean quality. Nor do markets consider earth's 'services', such as regulation of climate, detoxification of pollutants or provision of pollinators, much less questions of human equity and social justice. When water quality is degraded, well-off people can buy bottled water, for example, but poorer people cannot.

- A world conclave of 58 national Academies of Science agreed in 1993 that unchecked consumption and rapid population growth are likely to overwhelm technological improvements in affecting the environment.[5]

Clearly, the greatest environmental threat comes from both the wealthiest billion people, who consume the most and generate the most waste, and from the poorest billion, who may damage their meagre resource base in the daily struggle to avoid starvation. In addition, the billions in between are doing their best to increase their standard of living, in part through increased consumption.

- Although the world's supply of water remains constant, per-capita water consumption is rising twice as fast as world population. Humanity now uses more than half of the available surface fresh water on earth;[2] at least 300 million people live in regions that already have severe water shortages. By 2025, the number could be 3 billion.[6]
- The world's forests have shrunk from 11.4 to 7.3 square kilometres per 1,000 people since 1970. The loss is concentrated in developing countries, mostly to meet the demand for wood and paper by the industrialised world. Wild species are becoming extinct 50 to 100 times faster than they naturally would.[1]
- Over the last 50 years, 17% of the planet's soils have been severely degraded. That's nearly 2 billion hectares, the size of China and India combined.[1]
- The global emission of carbon dioxide, a 'greenhouse gas' most researchers say causes global warming and disruption in weather patterns, has quadrupled since 1950, largely from deforestation and the burning of fossil fuels. The atmosphere now contains 30% more CO_2 than at the beginning of the industrial revolution.[2] Where the industrialised world produces 60% of it today, the developing world will be producing 60% of it by 2015.[1]

Sources:

1 United Nations Development Programme, *Human Development Report 1998* (New York: Oxford University Press, 1998);
2 Jane Lubchenco, past president, American Association for Advancement of Science, speech: 'Women, Population and Science in the New Millennium,' Dec. 1, 1998, AAAS, Washington DC.
3 Ken Strom, *Population and Habitat in the New Millennium*, National Audubon Society and The Global Stewardship Initiative (Boulder CO 1998);
4 Population Action International, *Why Population Matters* (Washington DC: PAI, 1996);
5 Report, *Population Summit of the World's Scientific Academies* (Washington DC: The National Academy Press, 1993);
6 Simon, Paul, *Tapped Out* (New York: Welcome Rain Publishers, October 1998).

Developed by World Population Foundation and the Communications Consortium Media Center, with editorial contributions from the US NGOs in Support of the Cairo Consensus.
- The above information is from Zero Population Growth's web site at www.zeropopulationgrowth.org

Time running out for the environment

Information from the Johns Hopkins Center for Communication Programs

As world population continues to grow, natural resources are under increasing pressure, threatening public health and social and economic development, warns a new report from the Johns Hopkins School of Public Health.

'As we humans exploit nature to meet present needs, are we destroying resources needed for the future?' ask Don Hinrichsen and Bryant Robey, co-authors of the latest issue of *Population Reports, Population and the Environment: The Global Challenge*, published by the Johns Hopkins Population Information Program.

'Most developed economies currently consume resources much faster than they can regenerate. Most developing countries with rapid population growth face the urgent need to improve living standards' but risk irreparable harm to natural resources on which they depend, according to the report.

'Water shortages, soil exhaustion, loss of forests, air and water pollution, and degradation of coastlines afflict many areas,' write the authors. 'Without practising sustainable development, humanity faces a deteriorating environment and may even invite ecological disaster,' they note.

Sustainable development requires slower population growth. While the rate of population growth

has slowed over the past few decades, the absolute number of people continues to increase by about 1 billion every 13 years, and the environment continues to deteriorate. 'Can we assume that life on earth as we know it can continue no matter what the environmental conditions?' ask the authors.

The warning signs

Over the past 10 years environmental conditions generally have either failed to improve or appear to be getting worse, a review of the evidence finds. For the future, how people protect or abuse the environment could largely determine whether living standards improve or deteriorate, according to the authors. Despite international concern about the environment since the 1992 Rio de Janeiro 'Earth Summit', nearly every environmental sector is still cause for concern:

- Unclean water, along with poor sanitation, kills over 12 million people a year. Air pollution kills 3 million more.
- In 64 of 105 developing countries, population has grown faster than food supplies. Overcultivation, largely due to population pressures, has degraded some 2 billion hectares of arable land – an area the size of Canada and the United States combined.
- By 2025, with world population projected to be at 8 billion, 48 countries containing 3 billion people will face chronic water shortages. In 25 years, humankind could be using over 90% of all available fresh water, leaving just 10% for the rest of the world's plants and animals.
- Half of all coastline ecosystems are now under pressure because of high population densities and development. About half the world's population occupies a coastal strip 200 kilometres wide – just 10% of the world's land surface.
- Over the past 50 years nearly half of the world's original forest cover has been lost. Current demand for forest products may exceed the limits of sustainable consumption by 25%.
- Since 1950, according to one estimate, some 600,000 plant and animal species have disappeared, and currently nearly 40,000 more are threatened. This is the fastest rate of extinction since the dinosaurs disappeared.
- Over the past 40 years ocean surfaces have warmed an average of over half a degree Celsius, mainly as a result of carbon emissions from fossil fuel use and from burning of forests. Global warming could raise the sea level by 1 to 3 metres as polar ice sheets melt, flooding low-lying coastal areas and displacing millions of people. Global warming also could result in droughts and disrupt agriculture.

The report urges governments and policymakers to take immediate steps toward implementing sustainable development. Sustainable development means raising current living standards without destroying

the resource base required to meet future needs. In effect, the world needs to live off its 'ecological interest' rather than using up its 'ecological capital', the authors write. Steps toward sustainable development include using energy more efficiently; managing cities better; phasing out subsidies that encourage waste; managing water resources and protecting freshwater sources; harvesting forest products rather than destroying forests; preserving arable land and increasing food production – a second Green Revolution; managing coastal zones and ocean fisheries; protecting biodiversity hotspots; and adopting a climate change convention among nations.

Stabilising population through good quality family planning services 'would buy time to protect natural resources', according to the report. It would also provide opportunities for women and families to raise their living standards. The authors note that the number of people in developing countries who want family planning services has risen, but annual global spending on family planning programmes is less than half the US$17 billion agreed to for 2000 at the UN International Conference on Population and Development in Cairo in 1994. Developed-country annual commitments total just $2 billion – less than half the US$5.7 billion they promised to donate at Cairo. In the balance is whether the

world's population could eventually stabilise at 9 billion or less, or whether it will grow to 11 billion and even beyond. 'Just when it stabilises will have a powerful effect on living standards and the global environment,' write the authors.

Don Hinrichsen is a senior consultant with the United Nations Population Fund (UNFPA). Bryant Robey is editor of *Population Reports*. *Population Reports* is an international review journal of important issues in population, family planning, and related matters. It is published four times a year in four languages by the Population Information Program at the Johns Hopkins Center for Communication Programs for more than 170,000 family planning and other health professionals worldwide, with support from the US Agency for International Development (USAID). USAID administers the US foreign assistance programme, providing economic and humanitarian assistance in more than 80 countries worldwide.

- For more information about the Johns Hopkins Center for Communication Programs see their web site at www.jhuccp.org

© Hinrichsen, D. and Robey, B. Population and Environment: The Global Challenge, *Population Reports*, Series M, No. 15 Baltimore, Johns Hopkins University School of Public Health. Population Information Program, Fall 2000

The need for family planning

Information from the International Planned Parenthood Federation (IPPF)

Family planning is one of the success stories of development. Today, over half of all couples in developing countries are using contraception, whereas less than 10 per cent were doing so 30 years ago. Family size has dropped in most areas of the world, and in some countries by as much as a third. Consequently, the health of women and children has improved and the rate of global population increase is slowing down.

Most governments around the world are now convinced that family planning is an essential part of maternal and child health services, and accept the responsibility of providing contraceptive information and services. But there is still a long way to go before a wide choice of family planning services is universally available.

In spite of the progress that has been made, there are still hundreds of millions of couples worldwide who wish to plan their families but have no access to information or quality services. There are millions of unwanted pregnancies and the health of both mothers and children suffers when pregnancy is too early, too late or too closely spaced. Half a million women still die each year as a result of pregnancy or childbirth – as many as 100,000 of them from the consequences of unsafe abortion. And it has been estimated that 20 per cent of infant deaths could be averted if all births were spaced by at least two years.

The need for services will continue to grow: the number of women of childbearing age in the developing world will rise from 1 billion in 1990 to 1.5 billion by 2010. The challenge remains to provide family planning and reproductive health services for this increasing population.

Some segments of society require special efforts because their needs are often overlooked: young people, ethnic minorities and other marginalised groups, and the urban and rural poor.

The sexual and reproductive health dimension

It has been clear for some time that the health and well-being of women and their families improve when mothers are able to decide the number and spacing of their children. But there are a number of health problems and other issues related to sexuality and reproduction that concern people during the course of their lives, and the terms sexual and reproductive health have evolved to take account of such concerns.

IPPF recognised these additional needs when, in 1992, it adopted its Vision 2000 Strategic Plan. The plan, which was approved by all IPPF's member family planning associations, commits the Federation to adopting a sexual and reproductive health approach to its work. It makes promoting sexual and reproductive health as a human right and responding to people's sexual and reproductive health needs one of IPPF's six priorities for the 1990s.

Family planning services remain at the core of sexual and reproductive health care. But there are a number of other elements which are also considered important. These include:
- providing gender-sensitive information, education and counselling on sexuality;
- providing care during pregnancy, delivery and post-partum;
- monitoring infant growth and development with particular attention to the girl child and her nutrition, to ensure she grows up in an environment conducive to her development, including the development of her sexuality;
- taking care of people's concerns over sexually transmitted diseases and infertility;
- HIV/AIDS prevention.

The Cairo and Beijing conferences

In 1994, two years after IPPF's Strategic Plan was approved, the International Conference on Population and Development (ICPD) in Cairo gave an important impetus to IPPF's reproductive and sexual health agenda. This conference, which involved representatives from more

than 180 world governments, was a decisive one in that it firmly moved the focus of family planning away from fertility targets and national demographic goals towards meeting the needs of individuals for family planning and reproductive and sexual health care. The ICPD Programme of Action made it a goal for the world's governments to make available universal access to a full range of high quality reproductive health services, including for family planning and sexual health, by 2015.

The commitment to take action on sexual and reproductive health was reinforced at the Fourth World Conference on Women in Beijing in 1995. The Platform for Action recognised that the 'human rights of women include their right to have control over and decide freely and responsibly on matters related to their sexuality, including sexual and reproductive health, free of coercion, discrimination and violence'.

• The above information is an extract from the International Planned Parenthood Federation's web site which can be found at www.ippf.org or e-mail them at info@ippf.org

More women delay starting their families

By John Carvel, Social Affairs Editor

The changing face of family life over the past quarter-century is revealed in figures today from the office for national statistics showing a sharp increase in the number of women in England and Wales delaying having children until their thirties, or not having them at all.

Conception rates for women aged 20-24 fell by 20% between 1976 and 1998. For women aged 30-34 they rose by 62% and for those aged 35-39 by 82%.

In 1976, 69% of live births were to women in their twenties and 20% to women in their thirties. But by 1998, 42% of births were to women in their thirties while the figure for women in their twenties fell to 48%.

Mothers giving birth now are nearly three years older than their counterparts in the early 1970s. Last year the average age was 29.

The review of changing trends over the past 25 years also showed increasing childlessness. One in five 40-year-old women today is childless, compared with one in 10 of the same age in 1980.

The proportion of births outside marriage rose from one in 10 in the 1970s to one in four today. Of those births, under 8% are registered by the mother alone.

A trend towards cohabitation has grown steadily over the past two decades. The proportion of never-married women under 50 who are cohabiting has trebled to three in 10 over this period.

The national statisticians esti-

Population trends

- Births to women aged 35-39 up 82% over past 25 years
- Number of childless 40-year-olds doubles
- Proportion of women under 50 living with husband shrinks from two-thirds to just over half
- Proportion of children born outside marriage increases from 10% to 40%
- Unmarried couples expected to double to 3m by 2021
- Population of England forecast to reach 51.4m by 2008

---

mate there are more than 1.5m cohabiting couples in England and Wales and this number is projected to double by 2021.

Since the mid-1980s the proportion of women under 50 in England, Wales and Scotland who are married has declined from two-thirds to just over half. The proportion not living with a partner as a couple stayed fairly constant at about one in five.

The number of one-parent families rose from 750,000 in 1976 to 1.6m in 1996. And the number of children in one-parent families increased from 1.3m to 2.8m over the same period. Four out of 10 children were born outside marriage in 1999, compared with just one in 10 in 1979.

Abortions accounted for 16% of conceptions in 1976, rising to 21% in 1998. The proportion of girls aged 16-19 visiting family planning clinics increased from a minimum of 12% in 1988-89 to 22% in 1998-99. But the proportion aged 20-34 using these services fell from 21% to 12% over the same period.

The report included evidence of girls' earlier sexual activity. Among those born in 1931, 1% had first intercourse before 16, rising to 5% for those born in the 1950s and 24% for those born in 1974.

The national birth rate fell again slightly last year, with 622,000 live births, compared with 636,000 in 1998. If current fertility patterns persist, women are expected to average 1.7 children each – one of the lowest figures since wartime.

Women in the east London borough of Newham are the most fertile in Britain, with 92 live births per 1,000 women aged 15 to 44. The area with the lowest fertility was Cambridge, with 39 live births per 1,000 women.

In spite of the declining birth rate, the statisticians forecast that the population of England will rise from 49.5m in 1998 to 51.4m by 2008.

The fastest growing region will be London where the population is expected to grow from 7.2m to 7.7m by 2008, with particularly large rises in the north London borough of Barnet, and central areas such as Chelsea and Westminster.

Reproductive health and rights

Information from the United Nations Population Fund (UNFPA)

To decide freely and responsibly the number and spacing of children: this right is the key to better reproductive health for millions of women. It requires information, education and family planning services including contraceptives, prenatal care and prevention of sexually transmitted diseases such as HIV/AIDS. But in many places, people know too little about health and human sexuality, women are denied the freedom to manage their lives, and girls are expected to marry young and have children early – instead of attending school. These factors and others endanger the health and limit the potential of women and their families.

Reproductive and sexual health is a human right

- More than 585,000 women die each year from causes related to pregnancy, and perhaps 15 times as many suffer injury or infection. The odds of a woman dying from maternity-related causes ranges from 1 per 10,000 women in Northern Europe to 1 in 35 in southern Asia to 1 in 23 in Africa.
- Over half of all people who become infected with HIV are under the age of 25. Last year alone, 590,000 children and 2.5 million young men and women between 15 and 24 years old were infected. More than 33 million people are living with HIV/AIDS.[1]
- 70,000 women die each year from unsafe abortion, almost all in developing countries. At the ICPD, countries agreed to deal with the health impact of unsafe abortion as a major public-health concern. When abortion is not against the law, it should be safe.[2]
- Surveys from more than 60 developing countries indicate that more than 100 million women who are not currently using a contraceptive method want to delay the birth of their

> 'All couples and individuals have the basic right to decide freely and responsibly the number and spacing of their children and to have the information, education and means to do so.' – ICPD Programme of Action, Principle 8

next child or to stop having children.
- 50 million couples do not have access to a choice of safe and affordable contraceptive methods.
- Refugees, internally displaced persons and others caught in situation of conflict or emergency face particular challenges to their reproductive rights, from family planning needs to treatment and counselling in cases of sexual violence and rape.

When rights are respected, reproductive and sexual health improves dramatically.
- Over the past 30 years, the development of modern contraceptive methods has given people more freedom and ability to plan their families.
- Contraceptive use has increased from less than 10 per cent of couples 40 years ago to some 60 per cent of couples today.
- Family size has fallen from an average of six children in the 1960s to less than three.

- Up to a third of maternal death (mortality) and injury and infection (morbidity) could be avoided if all women had access to a range of modern, safe and effective family planning services that would enable them to avoid unwanted pregnancy.
- The opportunity to make a difference is multiplied greatly when the information, education and health care needs of young people are met. Programmes for adolescent reproductive health are a concern for UNFPA, community leaders, parents and young people themselves. Today, more than a billion people are between the ages of 15 and 24.[3]

Worldwide recognition of reproductive rights

The right to plan the size and spacing of the family was agreed to in 1968 in Teheran at the International Conference on Human Rights. In 1974 in Bucharest, the World Population Conference stated the following:

'World Population Plan of Action (Principle 14f): All couples and individuals have the basic right to decide freely and responsibly the number and spacing of their children and to have the information, education and means to do so; the

responsibility of couples and individuals in the exercise of this right takes into account the needs of their living and future children, and their responsibilities towards the community.'

Individuals and couples have the right to:
- Decide freely and responsibly the number, spacing and timing of their children;
- The information and means to make reproductive choices;
- Access to both family planning and related health services.

Sexual and reproductive rights include:
- Recognition that they are part of an overall lifelong health;
- Equality and equity for women and men in all spheres of life;
- Sexual and reproductive security, freedom from sexual violence and the right to privacy.

At the 1994 International Conference on Population and Development (ICPD), 180 countries endorsed a 20-year programme that protects the right to reproductive and sexual health. The ICPD Programme of Action affirms the rights of men and women to reproductive health care, including family planning and sexual health, without any form of coercion and the right to decide freely and responsibly the number and spacing of their children.[4] It asserts that reproductive health is a state of complete physical, mental and social well-being and not merely the absence of disease or infirmity, and implies that people are able to have a satisfying and safe sex life, that they are able to reproduce and that they have freedom to decide if, when and how often to do so. [5]

Goals of the ICPD Programme of Action
- Universal education – Elimination of the gender gap in primary and secondary education by 2005, and complete access to primary school or the equivalent by both girls and boys as quickly as possible and in any case before 2015.
- Mortality reduction – Reduction in infant and under-5 mortality

rates by at least one-third, to no more than 50 and 70 per 1,000 live births, respectively, by 2000, and to below 35 and 45, respectively, by 2015; reduction in maternal mortality to half the 1990 levels by 2000 and by a further one-half by 2015 (specifically, in countries with the highest levels of mortality, to below 60 per 100,000 live births).
- Reproductive health – Provision of universal access to a full range of safe and reliable family-planning methods and to related reproductive and sexual health services by 2015.

Five years after the ICPD, in 1999, world leaders met to review and appraise progress towards these goals. They focused on key future actions – steps that would best ensure that the goals of the ICPD Programme of Action would be met. Along with more attention to HIV/AIDS, issues that are urgent today include greatly increased numbers of both older and younger people, booming urban populations and rising international migration. Areas for action also include empowerment of women, poverty reduction, the environment, education for girls and the need for better data systems.

Examples of progress and success
- In Ghana, Uganda, Nigeria and Vietnam, midwives have been trained in life-saving skills, using a training package developed by the American College of Nurse-Midwives that includes risk assessment, problem solving and clinical management needed to save the lives of women during obstetric emergencies.
- In the years since the International Conference on Population and Development, two-

thirds of all countries have introduced policy or legislative measures to promote gender equity and equality and the empowerment of women, including the areas of inheritance, property rights, employment, and protection from gender-based violence.
- In Jamaica, early pregnancy forces thousands of girls from school, and few find jobs. With UNFPA funding, the Women's Centre of Jamaica Foundation provided vocational training and counselling services and helped many girls return to school. The aim: to break the cycle of poverty by emphasising a serious commitment to education and by helping young girls manage their sexual and reproductive lives.
- In Uganda and Thailand, the incidence of new HIV/AIDS infections, particularly in young populations, has declined by about one-third in response to intensive information and protection campaigns. Among adolescents, levels have reversed among young women appearing for prenatal care.

References
1 UNAIDS, December 1999.
2 Source: Report of the Ad Hoc Committee of the whole of the twenty-first Special Session of the General Assembly (A/S-21/5/Add. 1).
3 In many African countries half of all women have their first child before age 20, as do more than a third of women in much of Latin America. In the United States, about one in ten give birth before age 20.
4 ICPD Programme of Action, Principle 8, paras. 7.2 and 7.3.
5 ICPD Programme of Action Paras. 7.2 and 7.3.

Family planning

How family planning protects the health of women and children.
Information from Population Action International

Family planning dramatically improves the health and chances of survival of both mothers and their children. At the same time, when parents are assured of their children's survival, they may be more likely to plan their families. US foreign assistance should support both child health and family planning programmes because they are complementary. Together, these programmes contribute to improved maternal and child health, to family well-being, and to stronger families, communities and nations.

Too many deaths

Maternal and child deaths in developing countries are unacceptably high. Every minute of every day, a woman dies in pregnancy or childbirth and some 20 children die of largely preventable causes. More than 10 million children under age five die each year. In addition, an estimated 585,000 women die in pregnancy or childbirth every year, accounting for one-quarter to one-half of deaths to women of childbearing age. In some places, pregnancy is the leading killer of women this age.

Healthy mothers = healthy children

A mother's health affects the health of her children. To survive the vulnerable first few days and years, children need a good start in life. Women who are in poor health or poorly nourished are more likely to give birth to unhealthy babies and often cannot provide adequate care, diminishing the chances their children will survive and thrive. Breaking the cycle of weak mothers bearing weak babies gives both mothers and children a better chance.

The death of a mother is devastating for her family. Studies in Bangladesh show that when a mother dies after giving birth her newborn baby has only a small chance of surviving until its first birthday. Her other young children under age 10, especially girls, are also more likely to die. Children who survive a mother's death are less likely to receive adequate nourishment and health care. Older girls often drop out of school to care for younger siblings and do household chores.

Birth spacing improves child survival

The timing of births has a powerful impact on a child's chances of survival. Over the past two decades, survey after survey has shown that children born less than two years after the previous birth are twice as likely to die by age one than children born two to four years apart. When births are spaced less than 2 years apart, the risk of death before age five is two and half times that of births spaced three to four years apart.

Close spacing of births harms the health of mother and baby during pregnancy and forces children to compete for nourishment and maternal care. When a pregnant woman has not had time to fully recover from the previous birth, the new baby often develops too slowly and is born underweight or premature, increasing its chances of dying in infancy. Nursing a previous child during a pregnancy may harm the health of both children; the older child may also suffer if the new pregnancy precipitates early weaning. Children born close together have higher rates of malnutrition, develop more slowly, and are at increased risk of contracting and dying from childhood infectious diseases.

Teen pregnancies also at risk

Pregnancies to very young mothers also carry increased risks for both mother and baby. Children born to mothers under age 18 have a greater chance of dying before age five, compared with births to mothers aged 20 to 34. Babies born to very young mothers are again more likely to be premature or underweight. Teenage girls who are not physically mature are at greater risk of obstructed labour and complications during delivery. They are less likely to get prenatal care and to have the means to safeguard the health of their infants.

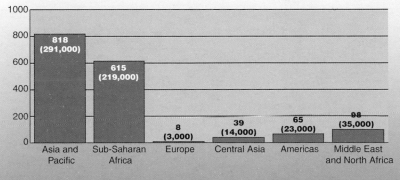

Deaths per day in pregnancy and childbirth

New estimates put the worldwide toll of maternal deaths at about 585,000 per year. When the 1990 data were revised, more than 80,000 maternal deaths were added to estimate. The graph shows an approximate number of women who die from pregnancy-related causes each day. The numbers in brackets show the annual number of maternal deaths for that area.

Area	Deaths per day	Annual deaths
Asia and Pacific	818	(291,000)
Sub-Saharan Africa	615	(219,000)
Europe	8	(3,000)
Central Asia	39	(14,000)
Americas	65	(23,000)
Middle East and North Africa	98	(35,000)

Source: UNICEF and WHO, January 1996 revised estimates of maternal mortality (chart in The Progress of Nations 1996)

Adolescent girls are also more likely to undergo unsafe abortions. Even where abortion is legal, access may be difficult for unmarried girls. Worldwide, at least four million teenage girls (15-19 years old) have unsafe abortions each year; in many countries the number of abortions to adolescents is growing and unsafe abortion is a leading cause of death among teenage girls.

Saving children's lives

Healthier patterns of childbearing could save the lives of several million children each year. By preventing closely-spaced births or those to very young mothers, family planning could reduce infant and child mortality by up to 25 per cent, or about three million deaths a year. Simply spacing all births at least two years apart could reduce infant and child deaths on average by 15 to 20 per cent. Moreover, improving patterns of childbearing requires access to effective contraception; while breastfeeding helps to space births, it does not provide reliable protection against pregnancy beyond four to six months.

The potential to save children's lives is greater where a high proportion of births are closely spaced. Improved spacing of births could reduce child deaths by a third in Egypt and Brazil. In sub-Saharan Africa, a smaller proportion of births are at risk because lengthy breastfeeding and sexual abstinence after birth help to space births further apart. But family planning is needed to protect child health as these traditional practices are abandoned.

Saving mothers' lives

By preventing high risk pregnancies, family planning could prevent at least one-quarter of maternal deaths. Girls under age 18, women over age 35, those who have four or more children and those who already have health problems are at greatest risk. In one area of Bangladesh, increased use of family planning significantly reduced maternal deaths among women of childbearing age simply by reducing the number of pregnancies.

Family planning can prevent many if not most deaths from unsafe abortion. Unwanted pregnancies result in about 50 million abortions every year, many of them performed under unsafe conditions. Each year, about 75,000 women die from unsafe abortions; tens of thousands more suffer serious complications leading to chronic infection, pain and infertility. Studies in several countries show that increased contraceptive use has contributed to dramatic declines in abortion rates, thereby reducing abortion-related deaths as well.

Family planning programmes help prevent the growing epidemic of HIV/AIDS and other sexually transmitted diseases (STDs) among women. Every year, over one million women contract HIV/AIDS; over 165 million contract other STDs that contribute to stillbirths and infant deaths. Family planning services can help educate women about safer sexual practices and encourage the use of condoms, the primary means of preventing these diseases.

A better future

A planned family is the best environment for a child's overall development. Studies show that unwanted children may suffer conscious or unconscious neglect. Parents with fewer children are able to devote more time and money to giving each child adequate food, health care, and education. Thus, family planning not only helps children survive, but makes it possible for them to develop their full potential and grow into healthy, productive adults.

More funds needed

Family planning is highly cost effective. According to the World Bank, family planning is one of the best ways to improve maternal and child health at an annual cost of only $1 to $2 for each person in the country. Yet family planning receives only a tiny fraction of health budgets and less than two per cent of all international development assistance. Recognising that family planning saves lives, strengthens families, curbs population growth and promotes sustainable development, UNICEF has declared that 'Family planning could bring more benefits to more people at less cost than any other single "technology" now available to the human race.'

French letters in the post

By Luke Harding in New Delhi

India's most populous state has hit upon a new way to spread the message about family planning and cut its booming population – the postman. Postal workers more used to delivering letters and parcels will now pop condoms and even the pill through the doors of residents in Uttar Pradesh's Agra and Ferozabad districts

The northern state has the same population as Brazil but, so far, all attempts to reduce it have failed, prompting exasperated chiefs at the Innovation in Family Planning Service Agency (Sipsa) to draft in 400 postmen to help.

The postal workers will gain an extra £1.50 a month for their efforts, plus a £1.50 'performance bonus', although it is unclear how that can be quantified.

Sipsa's chief, Anuradha Johari, said rural communities trusted postmen and viewed them as discreet, making it easier to talk to a postman about a personal matter.

Estimates suggest that only 5m out of the state's 170m inhabitants use contraception.

India's population officially shot through the 1bn mark in May, though most demographers believe it was passed some time ago. On current projections, the population could reach 1.25bn by 2016, and overtake China by the middle of the century.

China to relax 'disastrous' one-child policy

By David Rennie in Beijing

Twenty years after China approved its one-child policy the government is planning major changes to the way that the country's 70 million only children are brought up, as the long-term consequences of this unprecedented experiment in social engineering become clear.

The policy is to be softened now that the birth rate has dropped to safer levels. Zhang Yuqing, vice-minister of the State Family Planning Commission, said recently that the one-child system was 'a policy for one generation'. China has promised that, although family planning must stay, its enforcement will become more flexible, allowing for more categories of Chinese to be allowed to have more than one child.

State leaders, spurred on by a rash of student suicides, breakdowns and family murders, are facing up to the unbearable pressures faced by many lone children as they carry the expectations of their entire families on their shoulders. The policy has also coincided with the disappearance of millions of girls from the birth statistics.

According to the Chinese Academy of Social Sciences, 120 boys are now born for every 100 girls. In a few years, China will face a catastrophic shortage of women, with millions of men doomed never to find a wife. China blames illegal selective abortions, guided by the new technology of ultrasound. But the infant mortality rates are also heavily skewed: it is clear that infanticide, the historic curse of a nation where only sons may carry on a family line, is still widespread.

Girl-killing is not the only reason. Officials in the countryside, where most Chinese live, often allow couples to try for a second child, but only if their first is a daughter. Many rural families simply fail to register their daughters, instead paying a 'fine' to keep them.

Experts paint a gloomy future of sad and lonely cities. 'You cannot imagine what society will be like,' said Prof Huang Ping, of the Chinese Academy of Social Sciences. 'Old people are going to get more and more lonely, especially as the pace of urbanisation gets quicker.' The pressure on women to find a partner is intense.

> China has promised that, although family planning must stay, its enforcement will become more flexible, allowing for more categories of Chinese to be allowed to have more than one child

Openly single mothers remain almost unknown in conservative China, where a mere one per cent of 30-year-old women are unmarried. University students can be expelled for having sexual relations, let alone falling pregnant.

Officially, no woman can be forced to have an abortion. At the same time, a woman who falls pregnant by accident may not have an extra child. A mother who bucks the system faces huge fines and sterilisation.

Most seriously, she risks depriving her child of citizen's registration, condemning it to life as a non-person, with no right to education or hope of a good job. Even China's millions of registered Catholics are not exempt. The one-child policy comes above any individual faith. Members of China's official ethnic minorities are treated more leniently, and may have two children, or sometimes more.

Family planning abuses are one of the biggest causes of resentment in the countryside, where officials are accused of arbitrary terror — tearing down houses of peasants who break the rules, and demanding bribes from those who can afford to pay.

China first took steps to control its population in the Seventies, overturning Mao Tse-tung's disastrous calls for women to 'breed for the motherland'. After 1984, the one-child limit was largely abandoned in the countryside, partly to stem a wave of female infanticide.

State leaders, including President Jiang Zemin and the Prime Minister, Zhu Rongji, have now called on schools to produce more rounded, patriotic and 'sturdy' citizens.

Mr Zhu, a blunt economic reformist normally heard ordering shoddy state managers to shape up, told parliament this month that schools should 'reduce homework

assignments' and help children develop 'a spirit of innovation' and 'an appreciation of aesthetics'.

China's parliament, the National People's Congress, introduced the first formal one-child target 20 years ago this month, as an urgent response to a population explosion threatening to overwhelm the country.

Today, China defends the one-child policy, saying it had to take drastic action and that it has saved the world from having to feed an extra 300 million mouths. But critics condemn the policy for causing a nightmare of abortions, sterilisations, corruption and fines. Many Chinese would say both views contain some truth.

Germans urged to have more babies

By Hannah Cleaver

The Bavarian premier has called on Germans to produce more babies, breaking a national taboo on the phrase 'population policy', widely associated with the Nazi era.

Edmund Stoiber, leader of the right-of-centre Christian Social Union, the sister party to Germany's opposition Christian Democrat Union, said the word *Bevölkerungspolitik* (population policy), used by Hitler to encourage the production of blond, blue-eyed babies, must be stripped of its stigma.

'We have too few children,' he told *Die Welt* newspaper. The Nazis had abused the idea of expanding the population as an instrument of power. 'But for me it is not about having as big a German population as possible to outdo other countries.'

He gave warning of a demographic crisis for state pensions, caused by a low birth rate and an ageing population, and of other worrying consequences 'for our social network'. Government statistics suggest that Germany's current population of 82 million will fall by 17 million within half a century. This has forced the country to import skilled labour from abroad.

Mr Stoiber said an increase in immigration could ease the problem,

but not solve it. 'The level of immigration must be limited by the ability to integrate immigrants. Because of that it cannot be about increased immigration, but only about better administration.'

He proposed a set of official measures to reverse the population decline, including financial support

and tax breaks. But he said the main change must be made in people's attitudes towards children.

'We must make it the central point of our work. It is not just about money, it is about heads and hearts. When a young mother – like my daughter with her one-year-old son – goes to Italy and says she found it more child-friendly than here, something has gone wrong here.'

New generations and the family

Information from the United Nations Population Fund (UNFPA)

The family – the basic unit of society – is under stress as population continues to increase, the largest-ever generation of young people faces the challenges of adolescence, and a growing proportion of people pass the age of 60. High numbers and special needs define both young people and older people as 'new generations'. In addition, families are caught up in the rapid changes affecting many societies, including urbanisation, migration, globalisation and the spread of HIV/AIDS.

Impact of population size and structure

- More than 1 billion young people are between 15 and 24 years of age.
- More than 580 million people are over 60 years of age, and their numbers are growing at more than 11 million a year.
- Large increases in population size are projected in many countries for many years to come, despite recent declines in birth rates. With more than 6 billion in 2000, global popula-

tion continues to grow at 76 million each year.
- Population movements within and between countries, including very rapid growth of cities and the unbalanced regional distribution of population, will continue and increase in the future.
- Increases in the working-age population will continue until 2005-2010, but from then on, as older populations grow, the proportion of working-age people able to support the young and old will decrease. Between now and 2010, 700 million young people will enter the labour force in developing countries, an unprecedented 'demographic bonus' of human resources.

Less family support, more single-parent households

Around the world, family support networks are in decline and the proportion of single-parent-headed households is growing. Poor families are most vulnerable to the lack of social safety nets. The elderly and children have no choice but to work, parents are forced to leave their

children unsupervised and the birth of a child may result in a loss of pay or even in unemployment. In addition, women bear a disproportionate burden when they work outside the home yet carry most of the household work.

- In rural areas of sub-Saharan Africa, urbanisation often leads to young people being separated from their grandparents, who previously played a special role in the traditional education and socialisation of the young.
- In the Middle East, traditional extended households are gradually disappearing, as is the case in Egypt, where 84 per cent of all households are now nuclear families.
- In the United States, the growing number of female-headed households is one factor contributing to the feminisation of poverty in that country.
- In many countries, the HIV/AIDS epidemic is affecting the health and lives of young adults as they reach their most productive years; their orphaned children often depend on older relatives for their care.

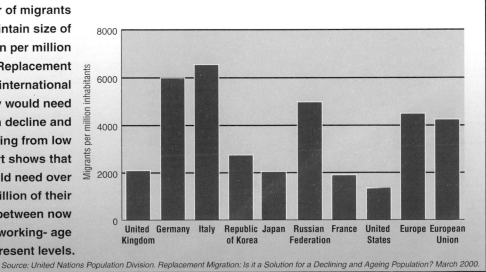

Migrants

Average annual net number of migrants between 2000-2050 to maintain size of working-age population per million inhabitants in 2000. Replacement migration refers to the international migration that a country would need to offset population decline and population ageing resulting from low fertility rates. The chart shows that Germany and Italy would need over 6,000 migrants per million of their population each year between now and 2050 to maintain their working-age population at present levels.

Source: United Nations Population Division. Replacement Migration: Is it a Solution for a Declining and Ageing Population? March 2000.

Young people's health and education issues

As the largest-ever generation of young people enters adulthood, education and information can affect when they marry, how many children they will have, and the well-being of their future families. For young women, the right to exercise greater control over their sexual and reproductive lives, free of coercion, discrimination and violence, is the key to a better future.

- Signs of discrimination are everywhere: the expectation of early marriage and pregnancy, the 2 million young girls who face female genital mutilation each year, the fact that only 76 per cent of girls compared to 96 per cent of boys receive some level of primary schooling and that among children who receive no schooling at all, girls outnumber boys.
- One in every 10 births worldwide is to teenage mothers. In least developed countries, 1 in every 6 births is to young women aged 15 to 19. Pregnancy before age 18 carries many health risks: girls age 10 to 14 are five times more likely to die in pregnancy or childbirth than women aged 20 to 24.
- Adolescent mothers will have more children than those who start childbearing later. Ultimate population size depends not only on the size of completed families but on decisions about when to start them – raising the mother's age at first birth from 18 to 23 could reduce population momentum by over 40 per cent.
- The onset of sexual activity marks the beginning of exposure to pregnancy as well as to potential health hazards, including HIV/AIDS. In most African countries, a large majority of women become sexually active during their teenage years – above 80 per cent in 16 of the 21 countries surveyed. In Latin America and the Caribbean, the age pattern is somewhat older. In more developed countries, the proportion of young women sexually active before age 18 is above 50 per cent.[1]
- At least 1 in 10 abortions

worldwide occurs among women aged 15 to 19. More than 4.4 million young women in this age group have abortions every year, 40 per cent of which are performed under unsafe conditions.
- Each day, 500,000 young people are infected with an STD – most in the 20 to 24 age group, followed by the 15 to 19 age group.
- Half of all HIV infections – 8,000 a day – occur in people under the age of 25. Girls are getting infected by older men: a new study supported by UNAIDS and WHO found HIV infection rates of 15 to 23 per cent among girls 15 to 19 years old, 26 to 40 per cent among men aged 25 or more, and just 3 to 4 per cent among 15- to 19-year-old boys.
- Unintended pregnancy early in life is usually the consequence of lack of access to information and services, unwanted sexual relations, unprotected sex or ineffective use of contraception. Unmarried pregnancy is often unintended. The unmet need for contraception is greater among sexually active young people than that of any other age group.

Actions to meet young people's needs

Specific actions can help young people avoid unwanted and too-early pregnancy, reduce recourse to abortion, prevent the spread of sexually transmitted diseases such as

HIV/AIDS. Moreover, respecting their rights to health and education will prepare them for lives as responsible and productive adults. Increasingly, young men are the target of efforts to promote responsible sexual behaviour and reproductive health. Programmes for young people endeavour to:

- Improve accessibility of health services and information;
- Offer sensitive and respectful counselling in a youth-friendly environment;
- Involve parents, teachers and community leaders;
- Increase sex education in schools and other settings (many studies have shown that sex education does not lead to promiscuity).

Services for an ageing population

More families can expect to have either elderly relatives or a child in the household. More people are living to older ages – 580 million people are over the age of 60 – with higher proportions of most countries' populations than at any time in history. Better medical care is preserving life at both ends of the age spectrum: infant mortality has fallen rapidly and more people are living longer. Combined with lower fertility, the effect is to increase the proportion of older people. This is what is meant by an 'ageing' population.

Better health, social and financial support services for ageing populations, and policy choices that support intergenerational equity will enable older people to remain healthy, independent and productive for longer. Public systems for old-age, disability or survivor support are now a feature of some 155 countries and territories, though their coverage varies greatly. Such services will also help families cope and enable older people to participate in self-help activities and in their communities. Not only must health care include sexual and reproductive health services, but emphasis should be placed on preventative health care to reduce the cost of curative medicine.[2]

References

1 United Nations, *World Population Monitoring 2000.*

2 ICPD Programme of Action, paras. 7.45 (young people) and 6.17 (older persons).

• The above information is an extract from the United Nations Population Fund's *Population Issues Briefing Kit 2000* which is available on their web site at www.unfpa.org

IPPF charter on sexual and reproductive rights

Introduction

The IPPF Charter on Sexual and Reproductive Rights is based on 12 rights, which are grounded in international human rights instruments, and additional rights that IPPF believes are implied by them.

It demonstrates the legitimacy of sexual and reproductive rights as human rights by applying internationally agreed language from human rights treaties, which have the status of international law, to sexual and reproductive health and rights issues. The 12 Rights in the Charter are:

1. The Right to Life, which means among other things that no woman's life should be put at risk by reason of pregnancy.

2. The Right to Liberty and Security of the Person, which recognises that no person should be subject to female genital mutilation, forced pregnancy, sterilisation or abortion.

3. The Right to Equality, and to be Free from all Forms of Discrimination, including in one's sexual and reproductive life.

4. The Right to Privacy, meaning that all sexual and reproductive health care services should be confidential, and all women have the right to autonomous reproductive choices.

5. The Right to Freedom of Thought, which includes freedom from the restrictive interpretation of religious texts, beliefs, philosophies and customs as tools to curtail freedom of thought on sexual and reproductive health care and other issues.

6. The Right to Information and Education, as it relates to sexual and reproductive health for all, including access to full information on the benefits, risks, and effectiveness of all methods of fertility regulation, in order that all decisions taken are made on the basis of full, free and informed consent.

7. The Right to Choose Whether or Not to Marry and to Found and Plan a Family.

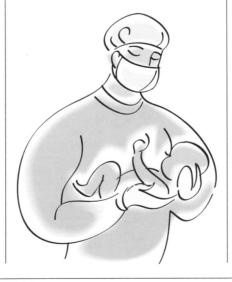

8. The Right to Decide Whether or When to Have Children.

9. The Right to Health Care and Health Protection, which includes the right of health care clients to the highest possible quality of health care, and the right to be free from traditional practices which are harmful to health.

10. The Right to the Benefits of Scientific Progress, which includes the right of sexual and reproductive health service clients to new reproductive health technologies which are safe, effective and acceptable.

11. The Right to Freedom of Assembly and Political Participation, which includes the right of all persons to seek to influence communities and governments to prioritise sexual and reproductive health and rights.

12. The Right to be Free from Torture and Ill-treatment, including the rights of all women, men and young people to protection from violence, sexual exploitation and abuse.

• IPPF works through more than 150 national family planning associations worldwide – and in at least 30 additional countries – for the sexual and reproductive health, choices and rights of women, men and young people. You can e-mail them at info@ippf.org

Speeding the reproductive revolution

Information from People & the Planet

By Bryant Robey and Ushma Upadhyay

For a very small price the reproductive revolution, allowing all children today to be born by choice not chance, with good health care, can be achieved in the first 15 years of the new century. But if that price is not paid, everyone will count the cost.

Six years ago, in Cairo, the world's nations set the goal of universal access to reproductive health care by the year 2015 and agreed to finance its costs. Imagine, then, a world in which access to care brought good reproductive health to all people:

- HIV/AIDS and other sexually transmitted diseases no longer plague the planet.
- Women have safe pregnancy and safe delivery of their children.
- Sexual violence is a thing of the past.
- Husbands and wives share responsibility for family health.
- All pregnancies are intended; all births are planned. People have only the number of children they want, when they want them.

Fertility falls. With lower fertility, other benefits follow: women have more choices and social, educational, and economic inequities by gender diminish. With fewer children, families can better feed, house, clothe, and educate their children. Healthier and better-educated young people become more productive, improving lives and speeding national development.

Pressures on natural resources and the environment diminish, while living standards rise. Adequate supplies of fresh water and arable land help assure ample food production, proper sanitation, and good health. Soon, development becomes sustainable.

Could such a world exist sometime in the future, or is it only a Utopia? There is reason for concern.

Few governments and donor nations have delivered on commitments made at the International Conference on Population and Development (ICPD) in 1994. Reproductive health is not improving, and it may be getting worse:

- More than 33 million adults and over 1 million children are infected with HIV/AIDS. Other sexually transmitted diseases (STDs) are on the rise; about 333 million new cases appear each year.
- Of the 175 million pregnancies each year, an estimated 75 million are unintended. In developing countries unintended pregnancies carry a health risk 20 times greater than the risk of using contraception.
- An estimated 585,000 women die each year from complications of pregnancy, childbirth, and unsafe abortion. Unsafe abortions cause between 50,000 and 100,000 women's deaths each year.
- Around the globe, between one-quarter and one-half of women have been physically abused by a sexual partner.

In developing countries an estimated 100 million married women of reproductive age are considered to have unmet need for family planning – that is, they do not want to become pregnant but are not using any contraceptive method.

While fertility has fallen in most countries, population is still growing rapidly, at almost 77 million every year, as estimated in 2000 – the equivalent of the current population of Vietnam. Continuing population increases of this magnitude, added to a population base already over 6 billion, would carry ominous consequences for the planet and its people in the future.

The 179 countries assembled at the ICPD agreed to an expanded reproductive health agenda, addressing not only fertility, family planning, and development but also reproductive rights, gender equality, women's empowerment, and men's participation. Country representatives agreed to some specific reproductive health goals to be reached by 2015, including:

- To meet all unmet need for family planning;
- To reduce maternal mortality by three-fourths compared with 1990 levels; and to reduce infant mortality to below 35 deaths per 1,000 births.

Far short of the goal

Reaching these and related reproductive health goals of the conference was calculated to cost about US$17 billion per year in 2000, rising to $22 billion per year by 2015 (in constant 1993 US dollars). Developing countries agreed to pay two-thirds of the cost; donor countries, one-third. While $22 billion per year represents a substantial increase over existing support for reproductive health, it is less than the world now spends on military expenditures in only 11 days.

Of the annual $22 billion, $14 billion would provide family planning information and services and improve the quality of care for over 600 million couples and would offer everyone access to safe and reliable contraception. Another $6 billion would support maternal health programmes and other primary health care related to reproductive health, including information and services for antenatal and postnatal care, emergency obstetric care, and treatment and counselling about STDs. And $1.5 billion would go for prevention of HIV/AIDS and other STDs through mass media and in-school education programmes, promotion of voluntary abstinence and responsible sexual behaviour, and expanded distribution of condoms.

Immediately after the ICPD, reproductive health funding by developed countries increased substantially but then fell back again, and is still uneven. In 1996 donor

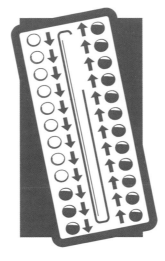

countries provided about $1.8 billion for population activities, $2.0 billion in 1997, $2.1 billion in 1998 and back down to $1.9 again in 1999. Funding levels are still only roughly one-third of the $5.7 billion target for developed countries. All together, expenditures for population activities yielded a global estimate of $10.6 billion in 1999, far short of the total $17 billion per year pledged by all countries in Cairo.

One might expect that reaching the ICPD goals would be easiest to achieve and fairest if the distribution of assistance among donor countries was relative to their ability to pay. Yet each country determines its own funding amounts, not according to the international need but to domestic priorities and politics. Most recent reports find in absolute amounts, the top three donors are, in order, the United States, Germany, and Japan. On a per capita basis, however, Norway, Denmark, Sweden, and the Netherlands contribute most, setting a world example.

Of the 175 million pregnancies each year, an estimated 75 million are unintended. In developing countries unintended pregnancies carry a health risk 20 times greater than the risk of using contraception

The United States, which has previously provided half of donor population assistance, has made cuts in recent years that have seriously set back efforts to achieve ICPD goals. Japan also does not appear to be increasing their funding. The United Kingdom has protected reproductive health and family planning programmes from recent budget cuts and continues to expand its population assistance. Belgium, Italy, and Spain, which historically have not provided population assistance, have begun to do so in a small way.

Multilateral sources, including the World Bank and regional development banks, agreed to contribute towards the donor-country target of $5.7 billion per year. The World Bank has adopted the ICPD agenda and is paying more attention to expanded reproductive health issues, instead of demographics. Still, the Bank could play a greater role, while other international banks could expand their health lending further.

Consequences of failure

The UNFPA has calculated the consequences for reproductive health of failure to deliver on promised financial support for the ICPD goals. Official assistance for 2000 has not yet been reported, but under the most optimistic funding scenario, in which the funding falls $2.1 billion short per year, the number of unintended pregnancies would be 42 million more this year – in 2000 – than if funders met their commitments. The number of induced abortions would be 17 million more. An estimated 99,000 more women would die of maternal causes in 2000, and there would be 1.2 million more infant deaths. Nearly 100 million people would be left without access to family planning information and services – a number equal to the current entire estimated unmet need for family planning.

Such dismal numbers would appear not only this year but would be repeated in 2001, 2002, and every year thereafter, as long as countries continued to fall short of the goal.

Obviously, these numbers would become much worse if governments and donor nations fell further short, while progress toward meeting the goal would save lives and improve health. Improved funding would also increase the availability of contraceptive methods, the number of programmes and projects carried out, the quality of services offered, and the amount of information that people could receive. Ultimately, failure to meet the goal would mean higher fertility rates and faster population growth, putting more pressure on the environment and making sustained development only an empty promise.

What can be done?

Countries at the ICPD did not intend to describe a Utopian world of the future but to set forth realistic and achievable goals for the international community. It is no secret that family planning and other reproductive health programmes work. Thanks in large part to family planning programmes, as well as other progress in development, fertility rates in

> *Thanks in large part to family planning programmes, as well as other progress in development, fertility rates in developing countries have fallen*

developing countries have fallen by nearly half compared with levels in 1960, while contraceptive use has risen from just one person in every ten in 1960 to about half of all women of reproductive age today. But what of the future?

Six years after the ICPD there is still time to continue the progress of recent years and, as promised, to expand the reproductive revolution. But governments still need to be convinced that paying for reproductive health programmes is an urgent priority and that developing

countries, donor countries, and multilateral institutions all have much to gain from reaching the ICPD goals.

Reducing human suffering and improving the quality of life is everybody's responsibility. Over the long run, increased national well-being also strengthens the global economy, international trade, political stability, and co-operation on such critical international issues as the environment, human rights, and security. Delay in meeting the ICPD goals means more problems in the future. The sooner the international community recaptures the spirit of the ICPD, the more the world can be a place future generations will be able to inhabit.

• Bryant Robey is editor of *Population Reports* and Ushma Upadhyay is research writer at the Population Information Program, Johns Hopkins School of Public Health, Baltimore, Maryland, USA.

© People & the Planet 2000 – 2001

Vasectomy

All you need to know about the kindest cut of all

1. Marie Stopes International (MSI) est la plus grande organisation non gouvernementale spécialisée dans la planification familiale.

2. Maintenant . . . whoops, sorry about that. Now MSI has come up with a nice little publicity coup to focus attention on its vasectomy service.

3. MSI is making a pitch for French custom, because vasectomy is illegal in France, under a 19th-century law forbidding 'self-mutilation'. Where that leaves French people with pierced ears is anyone's guess.

4. Statistics suggest that French people are rather more grown-up about reproduction than we are. Their teenage pregnancy rate, for example, is one-third the level of ours.

By Derek Brown

5. But French men who want to take contraceptive responsibility have only one option: French letters. But now, after using them for 15,000 years, they can book into MSI online.

6. A vasectomy is a five-minute procedure, performed under local anaesthetic, which involves cutting the *vas deferens*, the tube which delivers sperm from the testicles into the ejaculate.

> *A vasectomy is a five-minute procedure, performed under local anaesthetic*

7. To boost its so-called vasectomy tourist service, MSI has helpfully posted a list of *les questions les plus souvent posées*. One of the most common, in any language, is whether vasectomies can be reversed. (They can.)

8. Those who remain doubtful will just have to hang around for the male Pill. They may have to wait some time, though the International Planned Parenthood Federation reckons it might be available within five years.

9. Last year there was a bit of a scare story suggesting that vasectomised men had a greater chance of getting prostate cancer. That's since been debunked.

10. An MSI vasectomy costs £200. What's French for 'sounds like a snip'?

© Guardian Newspapers Limited 2000

Male pill is 100% effective in UK trials

By Paul Lashmar

Scientists at Edinburgh University said yesterday they had made a breakthrough in the race to put the first male contraceptive pill on the market.

They claim that tests show the version being developed at the university – which is already ahead of the field – appears to be 200 per cent effective and has no damaging side-effect. A six-monthly study involving 60 men in Scotland and China showed the pill had successfully made all the volunteers temporarily infertile.

The scientists say they are 'delighted' with the results. But birth rates will not tumble yet as they predict the male pill will not be on sale for five years.

Professor David Baird, a reproductive biologist and a member of the Edinburgh team, said the study was part of a programme aimed at providing a range of contraceptive options for men. He said: 'It is certainly very encouraging. We could have a male pill within five years. It could be as effective as the female pill, but more trials have to be done.'

The female pill is generally regarded as the most effective birth-control method – other than abstinence – with only one in 1,000 women using it becoming pregnant. But it can have serious side-effects and is avoided by older women.

This version of the male pill is being developed by the Dutch drug company Organon, which funded the trials in Edinburgh and Shanghai, as well as others in Cape Town and a small village outside Lagos in Nigeria.

The Edinburgh team is in competition with researchers at Strathclyde University in Glasgow and at Leicester University. At Strathclyde, the team is working on a once-a-year contraceptive vaccine. The injection works by attacking the sperm, ensuring they do not become mature enough to make a woman pregnant. Leicester's method relies on a chemical blocking the muscle actions that squirts sperm into semen.

The full results of the Edinburgh study will be presented at the World Conference of Gynaecologists and Obstetricians in Washington in September.

> **'It is certainly very encouraging. We could have a male pill within five years. It could be as effective as the female pill, but more trials have to be done'**

Professor Baird said the pill had none of the side-effects associated with earlier versions such as weight gain, high blood pressure, acne or loss of libido. It works by releasing hormones into the bloodstream to stop the body producing sperm.

The pill is made up of a combination of desogestrel, a synthetic steroid also used in the female pill, and the male sex hormone testosterone, which prevents a loss of sex drive. It convinces the brain that the testes are producing high levels of testosterone; brain signals to the testes are then switched off, and sperm production is halted.

The contraceptive could be developed as a tablet men would have to take every day to remain infertile. But because women might not trust men to take the pill daily it may be produced as an implant under the skin that gradually releases the hormones.

Birth-control scientists argue that the male contraceptive could be a valuable option for couples in their thirties and forties who do not want more children. Many men in such relationships either use condoms or have a vasectomy.

Population and reproductive health

Information from People & the Planet

Today, reproductive and sexual health is widely seen as a right for both men and women, and as a component of overall health, throughout the life cycle. This 'rights-based approach' was adopted by the international community at the International Conference on Population and Development in Cairo in 1994.

We now know that voluntary family planning has been very effective. Over the last 30 years, the percentage of couples in developing countries using family planning has increased from 10 per cent to 50 per cent. Access to family planning, coupled to economic development, has caused a marked decline in developing world fertility, from six children in 1960 to three today.

But it remains true that:
- One in four pregnancies in developing countries is unwanted and many more are unplanned;
- Every year, 50 million women have abortions to end unwanted pregnancies;
- Over 10 per cent of all births worldwide are to adolescent girls;
- Nearly 600,000 women die in pregnancy or childbirth yearly, greatly increasing the risk that their children under five will die as well;
- Over 2 million girls are subjected to female genital mutilation every year;
- Over 300 million people contract new sexually transmitted infections every year;
- Nearly 6 million people become infected with HIV every year;
- About 200,000 maternal deaths each year result from the lack or failure of contraceptive services.

Making a difference

Research has proved that good reproductive health programmes, especially when coupled with female education, have already made a major difference. Sri Lanka has reduced deaths among young mothers by 50 per cent. Family planning has made a big difference even in a poor country like Bangladesh.

HIV/AIDS, which is almost exclusively spread by heterosexual intercourse in the developing world, is one of the biggest challenges in the field of sexual and reproductive health, especially in sub-Saharan Africa.

The Cairo Conference also tackled three areas which previous international meetings had avoided or glossed over:
- Unsafe abortion;
- Violence against women, and in particular female genital mutilation; and
- Adolescent sexual and reproductive health – sexuality

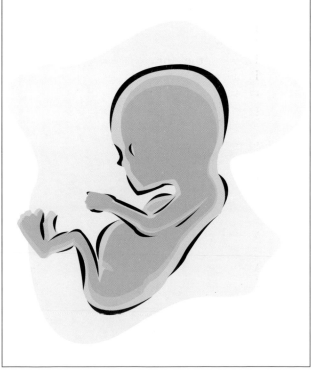

education and reproductive health services.

Adolescent sexual and reproductive health is perhaps the most urgent task for the international community. There are now more than one billion adolescents aged 10-19 in the world – and 85 per cent of them live in developing countries. These teenagers are tomorrow's parents. Their decisions about when to have children will have dramatic implications for their own well-being and for that of the planet. The outcome also depends on the quality of reproductive health services they receive. Better services could prevent millions of deaths among mothers and children; prevent hundreds of millions of abortions; and lead to lower overall population growth.

The great achievement of the Cairo Conference was that the international community recognised for the first time what many had argued for years:
- Coercion and demographic targets have no place in family planning programmes;
- There is a sufficiently high level of unwanted child-bearing in most developing countries that voluntary family planning programmes can readily attract contraceptive users and lead to significantly reduced fertility;
- Other reproductive health services, such as diagnosis and treatment of sexually transmitted infections (STIs) and infertility, should be provided alongside contraceptive services;
- Unsafe abortion is a major public health issue, best prevented by providing safe and effective contraception.

© People & the Planet 2000 – 2001

ADDITIONAL RESOURCES

You might like to contact the following organisations for further information. Due to the increasing cost of postage, many organisations cannot respond to enquiries unless they receive a stamped, addressed envelope.

International Food Policy Research Institute (IFPRI)
2033 K Street
N.W. Washington
D.C. 20006, USA
Tel: + 1 202 862 5600
Fax: + 1 202 467 4439
E-mail: ifpri@cgiar.org
Web site: www.ifpri.org
IFPRI's mission is to identify and analyse policies for sustainably meeting the food needs of the developing world.

International Planned Parenthood Federation (IPPF)
Regent's College
Inner Circle
Regent's Park
London, NW1 4NS
Tel: 020 7487 7900
Fax: 020 7487 7950
E-mail: info@ippf.org
Web site: www.ippf.org
The largest voluntary organisation in the field of sexual and reproductive health including family planning, represented in over 180 countries worldwide.

Population Action International
1120 19th St., NW Suite 550
Washington DC 20036
USA
Tel: + 1 202 659 1833
Fax: + 1 202 728 4177
Web site:
www.populationaction.org
Publishes the booklet *Why Population Matters*, also publishes many other publications on the issue of population.

Population Institute
107 Second Street
N.E. Washington DC 20002
USA
Tel: + 1 202 544 3300
Fax: + 1 202 544 0068
E-mail: web@populationinstitute.org
Web site:
www.populationinstitute.org

The Population Institute is the world's largest independent, non-profit, education organisation dedicated exclusively to achieving a more equitable balance between the world's population, environment and resources. Publishes the magazine *Popline*.

United Nations – Population Division
2 United Nations Plaza, Room DC2-1950
New York, NY 10017
USA
Tel: + 1 212 963 3179
Fax: + 1 212 963 2147
Web site: www.un.org/esa/population/unpop.htm
The Population Division is responsible for monitoring and appraisal of the broad range of areas in the field of population.

United Nations Population Fund (UNFPA)
220 East 42nd Street
New York
NY10017
USA
Tel: + 1 212 297 5279
Fax: + 1 212 557 6416
E-mail: hq@unfpa.org
Web site: www.unfpa.org
UNFPA, the United Nations Population Fund, helps developing countries find solutions to their population problems. Publishes *The State of World Population*, an annual report highlighting new developments in population. Also publishes many other titles and information on various aspects of the issue of population.

World Resources Institute
10 G Street, NE (Suite 800)
Washington DC 20002
USA
Tel: + 1 202 729 7600
Fax: + 1 202 729 7610
Web site: www.wri.org

World Resources Institute provides information, ideas, and solutions to global environmental problems. Their mission is to move human society to live in ways that protect Earth's environment for current and future generations.

Worldaware
Echo House
Ullswater Crescent
Coulsdon
Surrey, CR5 2HR
Tel: 020 8763 2555
Fax: 020 8831 1746
E-mail: info@worldaware.org.uk
Web site: www.worldaware.org.uk
Worldaware is UK-based and works to raise awareness of international development issues. For over thirty years, Worldaware has been a driving force behind the incorporation of development education resources into the school curriculum. Produces the publication *Global Eye* and the web site www.globaleye.org.uk

Zero Population Growth (ZPG)
1400 Sixteenth Street N.W
Suite 320
Washington DC 20036
USA
Tel: + 1 202 332 2200
Fax: + 1 202 332 2302
E-mail: info@zpg.org
Web site:
www.zeropopulationgrowth.org
Zero Population Growth is a national non-profit organisation working to slow population growth and achieve a sustainable balance between the Earth's people and its resources. We seek to protect the environment and ensure a high quality of life for present and future generations. ZPG's education and advocacy programmes aim to influence public policies, attitudes, and behaviour on national and global population issues and related concerns.

INDEX